Endorsements

Kids will love to read this book. I wanted to read the whole thing in one day.! I was encouraged to learn lessons about Jesus from kids my age.

Harper
A child of God

Julia's passion for Jesus, children, and helping kids deepen their relationship with Him shines through in this collection of devotions. *Hi God, It's Me Again* offers a relatable perspective on God's Word for any child, since it is written by children from diverse backgrounds. Our teachers love using this resource because it gives students the opportunity to hear God's truth through the voices of kids their own age, making it easier for them to connect with the lessons. This devotional book is a wonderful tool to inspire children to explore Scripture, understand its relevance in their lives, and begin reading and interpreting it on their own.

Owen Davis, Ph.D.
Executive Director, Santiago Christian School

A uniquely refreshing devotional from the hearts of children. Kids will enjoy the stories from other kids and parents will once again see Jesus through the eyes of a child. The hard part will be reading just one a day.

Allen Arnold
Director of Content & Resources, Ransomed Heart

This book will help every child develop Christ-centered responses to real-life situations. The unique, child-authored stories and application questions will inspire and encourage all children to think of others, not just themselves. Parents and teachers will use this book to stimulate meaningful worldview and respond to life circumstances rather than react to them. Homes, schools, and churches will find *Hi God, It's Me Again.* to be valuable and thought-provoking.

Don Hulin
Former Assistant Director of Textbook Development

HI GOD,

IT'S ME AGAIN

A Gospel Devotional
Written by Kids for Kids

BY JULIA TAVES

AND A TEAM OF CHILDREN
FROM AROUND THE WORLD

SECOND EDITION

Copyright © 2025 Julia Taves.

godlyencounters.com

Published by Abundance Books, LLC
Kalamazoo, MI
abundance-books.com

ISBN: 978-1-963377-33-0

10 9 8 7 6 5 4 3 2 1

Scripture quotations are taken from the Holy Bible, New International
Version®, NIV®. Copyright © 1973, 1978, 1984, 2011 by Biblica, Inc.®

Acknowledgments to Brian Mellema and Taryn Golliher for design and
Lindsay St. Gelais for editing.

Contents

John   157

Introduction

Children are curious characters. Listening to their thoughts gives voice to our inner hearts prompting us to ponder. Jesus welcomed children freely in his arms (Matthew 19:14). Scripture makes it clear that God has a special place in his heart for children. We are taught to emulate them in their humility; and we can learn a lot from how they approach God with trust in His goodness, even if things are difficult or confusing. "Truly I tell you, unless you change and become like little children, you will never enter the kingdom of Heaven." (Matthew 18:3-4)

This book has been written from the hearts of children. Children who are humbly seeking a Savior, Jesus Christ, in their young journey of life. This journey includes many relatable ups and downs. Yet, they have not been left to go the path alone. Jesus being the Way, the Truth and the Life has shown these children the way (John 14:6). Each devotion is a testimony to their humble trust, confirming key truths from the Gospels. Readers can journal and ponder about God and His Word also, affirming God's faithfulness.

Matthew

Part One:
Background to Matthew

Here's the thing: Matthew says, "Jesus is King!"

Matthew was one of the 12 apostles. These were men, chosen by God, who had witnessed firsthand and experienced Jesus' living, dying, rising from the dead, and changing lives. These men were chosen to make a difference in telling others about Jesus. Matthew is the first of four books telling this message. They are called, "The Gospels."

Matthew seemed like a humble kind of guy, who used to be a tax collector. Tax collectors were not very popular and were known to be cheaters in Matthew's day. Because of Matthew's sinful past, he was excited about the grace, forgiveness, and the love God showed to him. Throughout this book, he wrote about Jesus as the King, as well as Jesus' birth, life, miracles, teachings, resurrection, and finally concluding with what it will be like when Jesus comes again. The devotions you will read not only show how the disciples' lives were changed, but also show how kids' lives today have been affected by this "King Jesus" Matthew wrote about.

Star Struck

⁹After they had heard the king, they went on their way, and the star they had seen when it rose went ahead of them until it stopped over the place where the child was. ¹⁰When they saw the star, they were overjoyed.

Matthew 2:9-10

Have you ever had a time when you just knew God wanted you to do something? The Wise Men in Matthew 2:9-10 did. They knew God wanted them to follow the star to Jesus. And because they did, their lives were changed forever. They were so excited to give Jesus gifts to show their love to Him! God gives us opportunities to worship Him in giving also.

My birthday was coming up, and I was really excited to get presents. My birthday is near Christmas, so I am doubly blessed with presents! One day I was thinking about all the little kids who had to be in the hospital for Christmas. When I went to bed, I kept thinking about this, so I prayed about it. In the morning, I woke up and God gave me a great idea. I ran to my mom, told her my idea, and she loved it. At breakfast I told my idea to my family. My idea was to take all the money I got for my birthday to buy toys for the kids in the hospital for Christmas. Instead of getting birthday presents for me, I would go to the hospital and give Christmas presents to the kids there.

When the time came to give the gifts, they were amazed and loved each gift! It made me feel like I did something good and right. I felt inspired. God inspired me to do something amazing. On my birthday, I didn't have to go around telling everyone; it just blessed me to know I was helping others out of a love for Jesus! God would get the glory, not me!

Giving to those kids was like an act of worship to God, just like the Wise men did when they saw Jesus! What an honor it is to give what we have to Jesus the King.

By: Mariah (United States)

More from God: Matthew 2:1-12

Journal Prompt: Can you think of a time God inspired you to give to others as an act of worship to glorify Him?

Bad to Good

John's clothes were made of camel's hair, and he had a leather belt around his waist. His food was locusts and wild honey.

Matthew 3:4

John the Baptist lived out in the desert. That must have been rough. He wasn't like other people. People may have wondered why he ate locusts and honey and made his clothes out of camel's hair. That seems weird. To some people it may have seemed like a bad situation. John the Baptist had a greater purpose than having the right clothes and eating great food. Even though things may have been hard for him, God used his situation for good and helped him tell others about the coming of Jesus Christ, the Messiah. I'm sure he had to trust God to guide him each day.

Have you had a time where you thought something was bad and God made something good out of the situation?

One time when we were on our way to go camping, we had to stop because my mom had chapped lips. We wanted to get there and my brothers and I were all bummed that we had to stop to get some chapstick. When my dad got out, he noticed the tire on our camper was completely shredded and about to explode! Blowing a tire on a camper that is connected to an SUV can be very dangerous. We still had a long drive to get to our camping place. We looked and there was a tire store right around the corner. The store had the right tires! They told us we were very lucky we didn't have an accident. We knew it was God watching over us. We realized having a blown tire helped us to see God's protection and had a greater purpose. Sometimes you think God is putting you through something difficult when He's actually helping you learn to trust Him. Situations that are uncomfortable or different do not mean they are bad. God can work and guide you through whatever He calls you to go through to bring glory to Him.

By: Zak (United States)

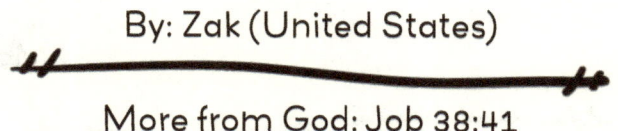

More from God: Job 38:41

Journal Prompt: How can you look differently at situations you are going through?

I'm Proud of You

16As soon as Jesus was baptized, he went up out of the water. At that moment heaven was opened, and he saw the Spirit of God descending like a dove and alighting on him. 17And a voice from heaven said, "This is my Son, whom I love; with him I am well pleased."

Matthew 3:16-17

Getting baptized shows everyone that you believe in Jesus and that He died for you and rose again. It is telling people you identify with him. This can be kind of ike wearing your favorite soccer team's jersey. When you have that jersey on, others understand you follow that team and want to be identified with them. When you are baptized, you are telling people that you are identifying with God and others see you as being with Him or following Him. Jesus did this as an example for us to do also. God was proud of Jesus for obeying.

Just as Jesus was baptized, I asked my parents if I could be baptized too. I wanted others to know that I am a child of God as I believe Jesus, God's Son, died and rose again conquering sin and death. I wanted to identify with Christ, obey Him, and have God be pleased with me.

God sent His son, who became the perfect man, and after a trip to Galilee, He got baptized. His Father was pleased with Him. Identifying with God and being baptized makes our Father, God, pleased with us too!

By: Anna (United States)

More from God: Matthew 3:13-15

Journal Prompt: Why do you think Jesus wanted His followers to be baptized?

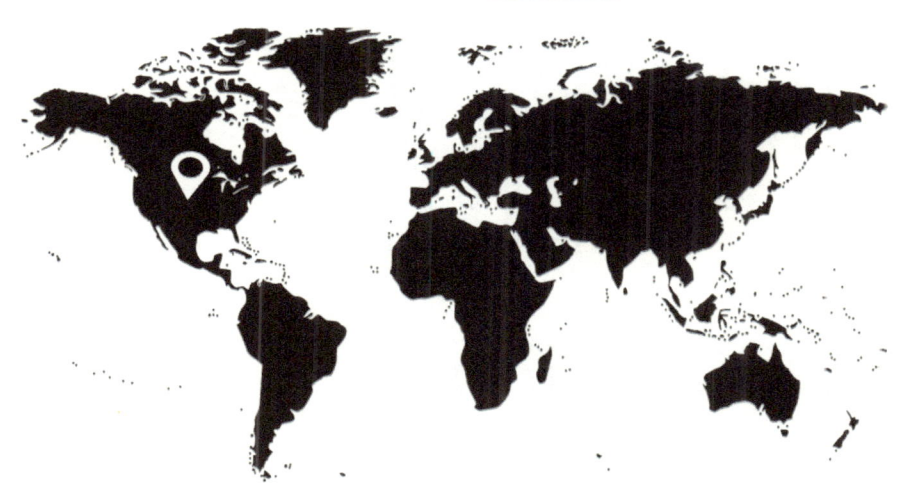

Temptation

¹*Then Jesus was led by the Spirit into the wilderness to be tempted by the devil.* ²*After fasting forty days and forty nights, he was hungry.* ³*The tempter came to him and said, "If you are the Son of God, tell these stones to become bread."*

⁴*Jesus answered, "It is written: 'Man shall not live on bread alone, but on every word that comes from the mouth of God.'"*

⁵*Then the devil took him to the holy city and had him stand on the highest point of the temple.* ⁶*"If you are the Son of God," he said, "throw yourself down. For it is written:*

"'He will command his angels concerning you,

and they will lift you up in their hands,

so that you will not strike your foot against a stone.'"

⁷Jesus answered him, "It is also written: 'Do not put the Lord your God to the test.'"

⁸Again, the devil took him to a very high mountain and showed him all the kingdoms of the world and their splendor. ⁹"All this I will give you," he said, "if you will bow down and worship me."

¹⁰Jesus said to him, "Away from me, Satan! For it is written: 'Worship the Lord your God, and serve him only.'"

¹¹Then the devil left him, and angels came and attended him.

Matthew 4:1-11

Jesus was tempted. I think this story is in the Bible because we should get through temptation just like Jesus did.

The devil tempts me too. Sometimes he tries to distract me from God. Maybe he distracts me from my devotionals or from praying. Maybe it's playing video games or going out with my friends instead of getting close with God.

Another way kids can fall into temptation is trying to be cool. Some kids only care about what the people at school or around their neighborhood think of them, not what God thinks of them. Sometimes when you want to be cool you do bad things. There are many other ways Satan tempts us too. One more way we get tempted is letting our anger out on someone. Perhaps we hurt them or say something offensive to them.

But we can resist temptation just like Jesus did. When the devil is tempting you to do something, a familiar Bible verse may pop into your head, and you will remember not to fall into the temptation. This is one reason it's good to learn memory verses.

Another way of avoiding temptation is having a right perspective of God. What that means is thinking of God as powerful to handle different situations.

For example: if your friends tell you to do something bad like cheat on a test, you might think, "My friends will think I'm cool if I do this so I'm going to do it," or "My friends might think I'm a little cooler if I do this, but God will give me strength to do the right thing." Go to God for help. He will be there.

By: Dylan (United States)

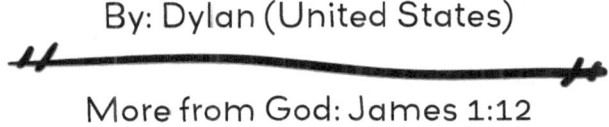

More from God: James 1:12

Journal Prompt: What do you do when you are tempted?

Mercy Matters

Blessed are the merciful, for they will be shown mercy.

Matthew 5:7

This is a situation that happened at school. The names have been changed, but I wonder if something like this has happened to you.

It all started at recess. "Tag!" Amy yelled as she tagged her best friend, Lilly. "I'm not even playing tag," Lilly said as she rolled her eyes. Amy then asked Lilly why she didn't want to play tag because Lilly usually loved to play tag. "Well, somebody is being pushy," Lilly said in a loud voice. Amy then yelled loudly, "I am NOT being pushy!" and ran away.

Later in the day, Amy felt bad and apologized to Lilly for yelling and running away. "Yeah, right," Lilly responded in a mean voice. Then Lilly saw the sadness on Amy's face, and she said, "Do you want to play with me at recess?" Amy agreed to play with Lilly at the next recess, but still had hurt feelings. She also felt bad about losing her temper and yelling at her friend. She didn't even know why they had a fight in the first place! Then she prayed and asked Jesus to help her show mercy and forgive her friend. Jesus did just that! Lilly not only played with Amy the next day, but she also let her be "it" first.

Jesus wants us to show mercy and compassion to everyone, even those who are unkind. Just as Jesus showed mercy to us by forgiving all our sins when He died on the cross, so we should show that to others. Those who are merciful will receive mercy themselves from God.

By: Sophia (United States)

More from God: 1 Peter 3:8

Journal Prompt: Think about someone you could show mercy to. What will you do to show them mercy?

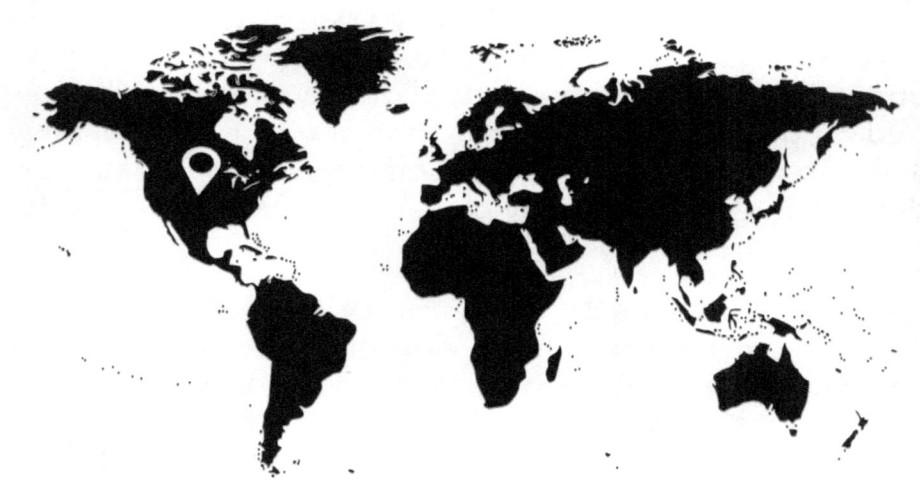

Gift Bags

In the same way, let your light shine before others, that they may see your good deeds and glorify your Father in heaven.

Matthew 5:16

Letting your light shine and doing good deeds feels good. I experienced this firsthand. During the Waldo Canyon Fire in Colorado, firefighters from North Carolina, Wyoming, and California came to give aid. These "hotshot" firefighters work very hard with not much sleep or food to eat for 12 to 13 hours a day.

My dad is one of these firefighters, and his job is to fly planes and drop fire retardants on places where the wildfires are extremely hot! This made me start thinking. I said, "Mom, can we make goodie bags for people at daddy's work?" Mom agreed.

Our house turned into a donation center. We got one or two deliveries each day. We went every Friday to hand the baggies out. While I was there, I got to see the firefighters in action and the red stuff they dropped on the fire. Lots of kids made cards and decorated bags for my dad's crew. One of our friends made some C130's (airplane) using Rollo candy and colored sticks. It was so much fun!

One time when we delivered the bags, all the people literally ran into the break room to get one! They saw the good deeds God asked us to do and were blessed by it! I saw God using me to help others. I know God is glorified when we let His light shine for others that He might be honored in what we do.

By: Faith (United States)

More from God: Acts 20:35

Journal Prompt: When was a time you let your light shine to do a good deed so God could be glorified?

Me? Love My Enemies?

But I tell you, love your enemies and pray for those who persecute you

Matthew 5:44

It doesn't feel too great when someone teases you. It seems like I get teased 24-7! Can you guess who does the most teasing in my life? It is my own sister! Normally you would think that I'd be mean back. Now I'm not perfect, but I really try to be nice to her even when she is not nice to me. It really works most of the time. I'll give you an example.

One time before school, I got up early and made my sister lunch for her to take so she wouldn't have to do that. She loved it, and the kindness I showed really changed her attitude. I guess just showing love to someone who seems like your enemy can go a long way.

Whether it is a sister, brother, classmate, teammate, or neighbor teasing you or not being kind, try asking God to help you think of something nice to show love to them. It will not only change their attitude, but yours also. God's Word really does make a difference when you apply it.

By: Brian (United States)

More from God: Proverbs 25:21-22

Journal Prompt: Think of some way to love someone who has not been kind to you. Journal about it.

My Closet

⁵And when you pray, do not be like the hypocrites, for they love to pray standing in the synagogues and on the street corners to be seen by others. Truly I tell you, they have received their reward in full. ⁶But when you pray, go into your room, close the door and pray to your Father, who is unseen. Then your Father, who sees what is done in secret, will reward you.

Matthew 6:5-6

Have you ever prayed in secret? I have. Jesus says in the Bible to go to your room and close the door to pray, and then God will reward you in the glorious kingdom of heaven.

Sometimes when I pray, I am in my room, but not always. I like being by myself when I talk to God. It is quiet and I can just think about Him. I know He is there with me.

Sometimes I get a piece of paper and write down my prayer. Just spending time with God is great!

Next time you pray, go to your room, and think about spending some quiet time with God. You can always count on God to be with you during your special time alone with him.

By: Emily (United States)

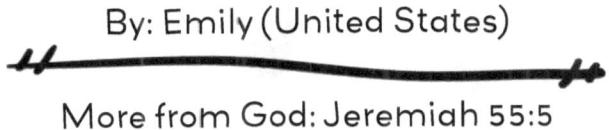

More from God: Jeremiah 55:5

Journal Prompt: When was the last time you spent time alone praying with God? Where can you go to do that?

Does God Hear Me?

9"This, then, is how you should pray:

"'Our Father in heaven, hallowed be your name,
10your kingdom come, your will be done, on
earth as it is in heaven. 11Give us today our daily
bread. 12And forgive us our debts, as we also
have forgiven our debtors. 13And lead us not into
temptation, but deliver us from the evil one.

Matthew 6:9-13

Do you ever talk to God? We can talk to God anytime as Jesus, God's son, taught us how to pray. We can talk to God alone or with others.

When I pray with my family I tell God, "We love you, God, with everything we've got, everything we do and everything we don't do." Also, praying Psalm 4:8 at bedtime helps me to feel safe and not afraid. I pray before meals to thank God for my food. I pray for other people who are sick because it's good to care for others. I pray at church. I pray when I need to tell God I'm sorry because I have disobeyed. That makes me feel better because God forgives me.

Sometimes I pray by singing and dancing to God. Other times I talk to God quietly in my head. God hears me when I am happy, sad, worried, tempted, or concerned for others. It is awesome to just tell Him about things I need or am wondering. Mostly, I can praise Him as He is a Holy, awesome God.

If God's son, Jesus, taught us to pray, you know He is listening and cares. It is amazing to think the God of the universe wants a relationship with us. He longs to talk to us! You can pray in Jesus' name and know God hears you.

Inspired by Ruby (United States)

More about God: Psalm 5:3

Journal Prompt: Write a prayer to God. He is listening!

Shot With Anger

¹⁴*For if you forgive other people when they sin against you, your heavenly Father will also forgive you.* ¹⁵*But if you do not forgive others their sins, your Father will not forgive your sins.*

Matthew 6:14-15

Have you ever been really angry? I was once. It was one night when my dad and I were spending quality time together. We like to play around and have fun teasing each other. This night I had a nerf gun waiting to play nerf war with my dad. I was sitting on the couch, and I went up to get a snack.

My dad thought that it would be funny if he spooked me with the nerf gun, so he surprised me and fired. He meant to just scare me, but accidentally hit me at closer range than I expected! (I guess his aim was better than he thought!) At first, I felt like getting mad and stomping off, even though I was not really hurt. Well, I actually was going to do that; but instead, I thought differently and decided not to get angry.

My dad said he was sorry and I forgave him. The lesson is I was angry for a second, but cooled off and did the right thing. So, if you do get angry, remember to forgive because Jesus forgives you. That is the way God wants us to handle it when others do something against us. It feels much better to do that. My dad and I had a great night together even though it started that way. Forgiving others is so much better than staying mad!

By: Luke (United States)

More from God: Ephesians 4:26

Journal Prompt: Can you write about a time you forgave instead of staying angry?

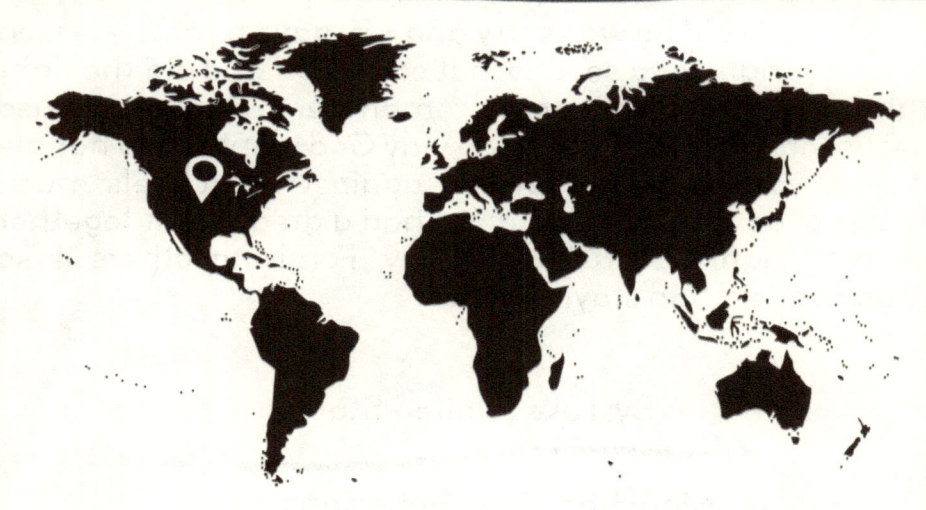

Being Worried

Therefore I tell you, do not worry about your life...

Matthew 6:25a

Have you ever been worried about anything? When I went to my cousin's Navy SEALS graduation in California, I was definitely worried. The graduation ceremony was impressive. My cousin said it was so tough to make it through the courses to graduation. Afterward, he told us he had to learn Swahili, which is an African language, and then go to Africa on a mission in June.

I was so worried because it seemed far way and unknown. I thought we might never see him again after we left California! I knew I would really miss him a lot. God was going to teach me through Matthew 6:25 not to worry about stuff as much.

The next day we left California. When we took off, I was trying not to, but I was still feeling anxious about it. When we got back to Colorado, my dad taught me Matthew 6:25.

It helped me not to be as worried as I used to be. Then, when June came, my cousin left.

God helped me not to be so worried anymore. I know He is with my cousin and with me too. God has helped me to trust in him more each day.

By: Jimmy (United States)

More from God: 2 Thessalonians 3:16

Journal Prompt: How would remembering Matthew 6:25 help you?

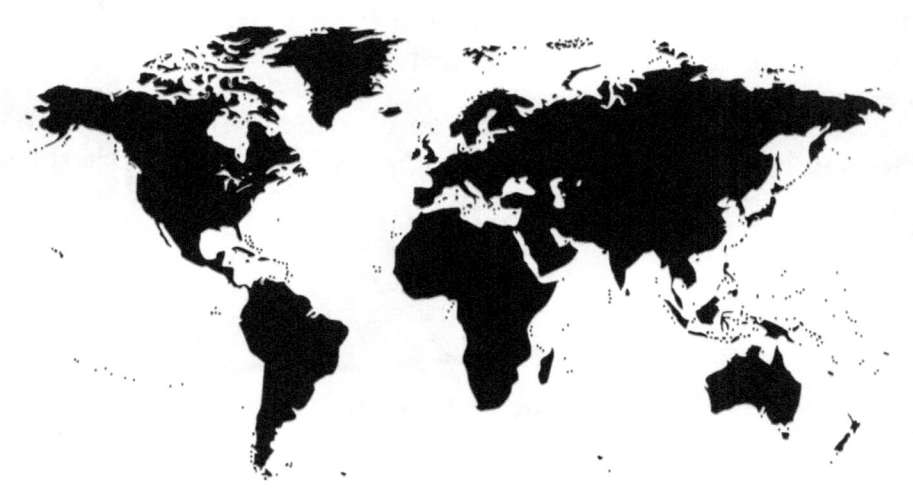

Looks Over Books

²⁵Therefore I tell you, do not worry about your life, what you will eat or drink; or about your body, what you will wear. Is not life more than food, and the body more than clothes? ²⁶Look at the birds of the air; they do not sow or reap or store away in barns, and yet your heavenly Father feeds them. Are you not much more valuable than they? ²⁷Can any one of you by worrying add a single hour to your life?

Matthew 6:25-27

I am in fifth grade right now and in fifth grade you often care about things that you have never cared about before. Sometimes it can get a little crazy worrying about wearing the right clothes to make an impression on others. It can be overwhelming.

This year I was in class with a girl who got a lot of attention due to her looks. Jealousy took over me. This ate me up inside, so I tried to step up my game by buying new clothes. All of this consumed me so much that I forgot we had a science test coming up. One night my mom asked me if I had any homework and I said, "No" because I forgot about the test. That day we went shopping and spent a lot of money to buy cute clothes.

So, the next day I wore my new outfit, but when I got to school everyone was crowded around that girl! (OF COURSE!) I walked up in my new, expensive outfit, and everyone had their books open. "What?" I said to myself, "Why do they have their books open?" I sat down at the table, and then remembered... the science test!!! I got my book out of my backpack and went through it as fast as I could. A few minutes later the bell rang, and boy, was my heart beating! I walked to the class with my face stuck in the book! I got to my locker and brought my book inside the class, looked on the board and there it was in black dry erase marker... Science Test! When it came time for the test, I was so scared! I wrote my name on the top and hoped that I would do a good job, but when I got it back, I wasn't happy because I got a pretty bad grade!

This story shows how you should not make looks more important than anything, especially not the Bible and your relationship with Jesus! God will take care of your clothes, and external things. The beauty inside a person is important to God. Focusing on other things besides Him, whether it is clothes, or whatever, will only cause heartache. Your value comes from God.

By: Anonymous

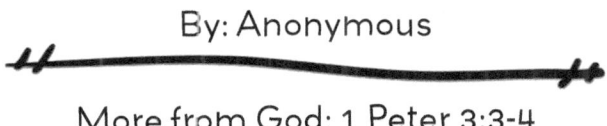

More from God: 1 Peter 3:3-4

Journal Prompt: Have you ever worried if you were pretty or handsome enough? If you have, pray about it, and ask God to help you see where your value comes from.

The Small and Lonely Feather

Look at the birds of the air; they do not sow or reap or store away in barns, and yet your heavenly Father feeds them. Are you not much more valuable than they?

Matthew 6:26

Once I was outside in my backyard playing by some rocks. I noticed something in the rocks that was all wet. I figured it was something that had fallen from the hailstorm which had occurred the previous day. To get a better look I bent down and investigated. I carefully looked and it was feathers lying in the rocks. I then noticed one feather that was small and separated from the rest. This feather was different from the rest because it was not damaged but seemed to be in perfect shape! I was in awe at the pretty colors and yellow and black designs God had made on the bird's feather. Then I felt sad that the little bird had lost such a pretty feather. Even though some feathers were on the ground, it seemed the bird had survived the storm and had flown away.

Then I thought about how much God loved that little bird to make him with such cool feathers for protection. Just as God shows us how birds are valuable to Him by the way He made them and cares for them, so He values us even more! I am thankful God showed this to me. He made me special, just like that bird and He values, protects, and cares for me. The next time I am worried I can think about how God will take care of me when I am going through one of life's storms, just like He did for that little bird.

By: Maddie (United States)

More from God: Jeremiah 29:11

Journal Prompt: Think of ways God shows His love and care for you.

Butterflies in the Air

Therefore do not worry about tomorrow, for tomorrow will worry about itself. Each day has enough trouble of its own.

Matthew 6:34

Have you ever felt so nervous that you thought you had butterflies in your stomach as well as flying around you in the air? It happened to me once when I was playing my first volleyball game.

It was nerve-racking. I was working hard in the first game just passing and playing left front. We were up against a tough rival. My friend Abby was serving first. It went over and the other team tried to pass it back, but with no success. When I was about to serve for the first time, I was nervous. The referee blew the whistle and I started to say in my mind Philippians 4:13, "I can do all things through Christ who strengthens me." When I did that, I felt as if I had a whole lot of strength in me. When I served the ball, it went over! I couldn't believe it! Then the coach subbed me out.

Later I went back in and when it was my turn to serve the second time, it was going to be the winning point for our team. God gave me strength, and I scored the winning point! We all were screaming. We had to all go to the end line of the volleyball court and run and clap hands with the opponent and say, "Good game or good job." Once that was over, we all celebrated.

Remembering God's Word gave me strength and helped me not to worry. It is great that we won, but trusting in God's plan and outcome does not always mean winning the game. God's Word will give you strength when you are nervous or afraid and help you focus on Him. God shows us His glory in the midst of our insecurities.

By: Mary (United States)

More from God: John 14:27

Journal Prompt: Name a time when you were nervous. How did God help you?

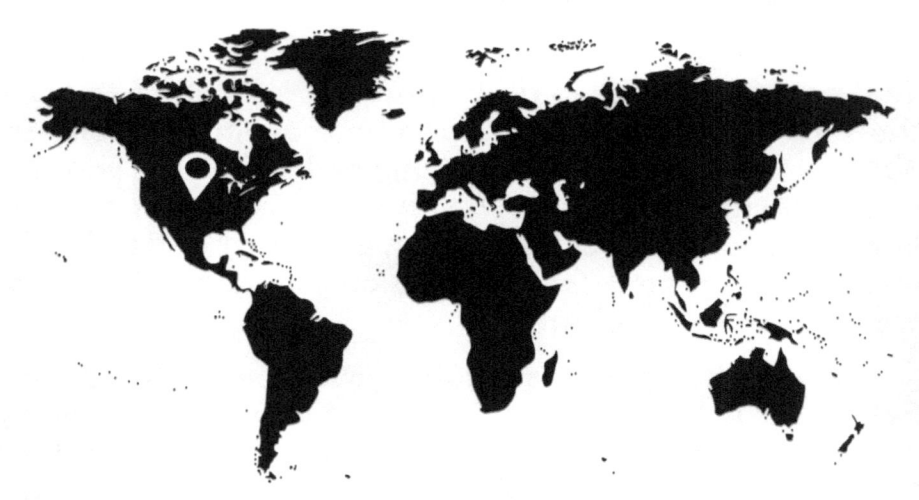

Legos

24"Therefore everyone who hears these words of mine and puts them into practice is like a wise man who built his house on the rock. 25The rain came down, the streams rose, and the winds blew and beat against that house; yet it did not fall, because it had its foundation on the rock. 26But everyone who hears these words of mine and does not put them into practice is like a foolish man who built his house on sand. 27The rain came down, the streams rose, and the winds blew and beat against that house, and it fell with a great crash."

Matthew 7:24-27

Did you know that Lego structures and lives are a lot alike? Sure, people are not plastic, but people's lives and Lego structures both need a strong, solid base.

One way our lives are like Legos is that they both have

directions. People that make the Legos have a plan for what the creation will be. God has a plan for us too. He planned for what you would be and do even before you were born.

I built a Lego ship once. It turned out really coo. My ship was not perfect, though, because I did not follow the directions, so as I played with it the ship fell apart. It is the same with our lives. If we do not follow God and do what He would have us do, our lives will fall apart just like my ship did. We cannot control everything, but God can. He is in control. God knows best and is always right so if we use His directions for our life we cannot go wrong.

Whenever I build with Legos, I have to be able to recognize the pieces and know what they are for. Flat pieces are good at holding things together and tall ones are good for walls. It is the same with our lives. God puts lots of different people in our lives to help us serve His purpose. Some friends or family may be servants, some prayer warriors, and other encouragers. If everyone works together in the body of Christ, the body can be strong and amazing just like a huge strong Lego structure.

The only great "base" we can get in our lives is from following and answering God. If we do not let God give us our base, the "pieces" of our lives will not fit together and will eventually crumble. As we read our Bible, pray, and serve together in the body of Christ, our "base" will grow stronger.

By: Ethan (United States)

More from God: Matthew 7:21-23

Journal Prompt: How has God put you and me together to help others in the body of Christ?

Faith

Trusting God during hard times and having faith can really be hard. Before I was born, my mom had cancer, even when I was in her tummy. My parents had to wait 9 months to see if the cancer went away. They had to have faith in God. My parents were in Germany while my dad was in the military and could not just go home.

While my mom was lying in bed, she prayed. God gave her some great adventure in trusting Him. Later, when I was born, the doctors realized my mom did not have cancer anymore!

My parents were thinking what to name me and decided to call me "Faith" because they had to have faith in God through hard times before I was born. God brought me into the world, and it took faith for my parents to trust in God for my mom's health and the miracle of my birth. God was faithful as they waited on Him for healing and the future (Matthew 8:14-15).

By: Faith (United States)

More from God: Hebrews 11:1

Journal Prompt: Write about a difficult time when God was faithful.

Car Crash Dilemma

He replied, "You of little faith, why are you so afraid?" Then he got up and rebuked the winds and the waves, and it was completely calm.

Matthew 8:26

Bad things happen sometimes, even to loved ones! It was a spring afternoon when I was doing homework. The phone rang; my dad picked it up. When he picked it up, there was a long pause of silence. He had a concerned look on his face.

It was my mom. It seems that on the way home from Denver she had gotten in a major car crash! My dad immediately left to pick her up. But I was calmer than I usually would be.

Eventually I came to know that it wasn't just a random boost of self-control. I knew God was with me that day and helped me not freak out and keep my cool. Also, my mother had not suffered any major injuries, just some minor soreness in the neck and back.

God brought to mind the verse Matthew 8:26 to think about through this trial. Jesus took care of the disciples when they were in the middle of the storm in their boat. I would have been very afraid during that! He helped me through my storm and He will do this for you also. When you feel like you're getting scared just remember that God is with you.

By: Luke (United States)

More from God: Philippians 4:6

Journal Prompt: Think of a time you became afraid. Write a verse that comes to mind for help.

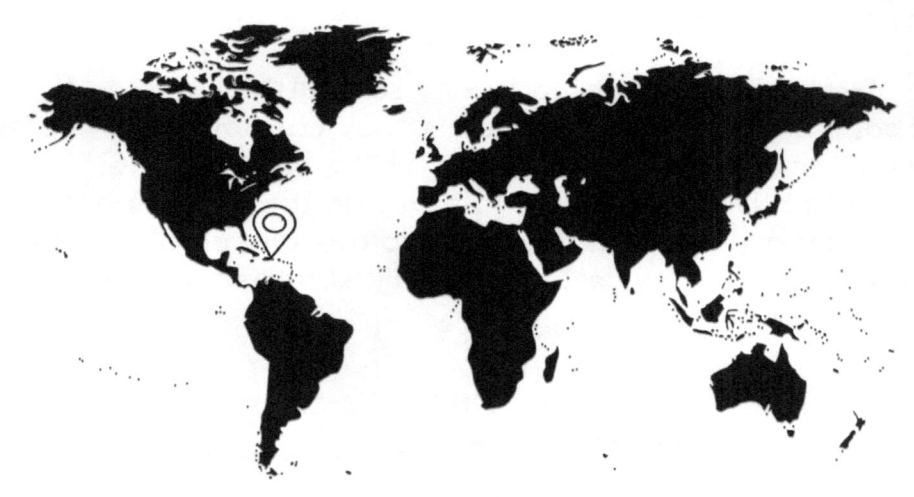

God Loves Me

Come to me, all you who are weary and burdened, and I will give you rest.

Matthew 11:28

It all started with a little 4 year old girl named Azul, which is me. I was going to a new preschool, and I was learning about God. It really amazed me all the things God can do. It's really cool that at that early age I was learning so much about God. I continue learning in that school.

One day I learned that God loves us a lot and wants to know us and help us such as in the verse "Come to me all who are tired and I will give you rest." Matthew 11:28

God wants us to be joyful and rest in His presence, we are not perfect, but he is.

Always remember God loves you just by who you are because He made you. He knows everything about you. If you wear glasses and if you have dark skin or brown hair. He knows about the size of your body, but what he cares most about is what is in your heart. When we are tired or worried about things God is there for us and carries us through.

God knows you, loves you and cares about you. You can rest in Him.

Azul (Dominican Republic)

More about God: Jude 23-24

Journal Prompt: What are you learning about God?

What's In Your Heart?

³⁴You brood of vipers, how can you who are evil say anything good? For the mouth speaks what the heart is full of. ³⁵A good man brings good things out of the good stored up in him, and an evil man brings evil things out of the evil stored up in him.

Matthew 12:34-35

When I was younger, I thought that I had better things than everybody. I always bragged and only thought about myself. What came out of my mouth was from my heart. But they weren't good things.

Later, when I filled my heart with God's Word, things changed. I stopped thinking about myself and comparing what I had with others. God helped me to start putting others first. (James 4:1-8) I realized that Jesus is the good in me and I don't have to brag about myself. Any good that comes from me is Jesus in me.

Now, when I see someone who is in need and I can help, I try to help them. It gives me true joy to give something to someone else. I give freely instead of keeping things for myself. I realize that everything I have been given comes from God, not me. God and His Word changed my heart, and it can change yours too!

By: Angelina (United States)

More from God: Jeremiah 17:9-10

Journal Prompt: What causes arguments, and bad things to come out of your mouth? Read James 4:1-4 to find the answer.

Trust in God

²⁸"Lord, if it's you," Peter replied, "tell me to come to you on the water."

²⁹"Come," he said.

Then Peter got down out of the boat, walked on the water and came toward Jesus. ³⁰But when he saw the wind, he was afraid and, beginning to sink, cried out, "Lord, save me!"

³¹Immediately Jesus reached out his hand and caught him. "You of little faith," he said, "why did you doubt?"

³²And when they climbed into the boat, the wind died down. ³³Then those who were in the boat worshiped him, saying, "Truly you are the Son of God."

Matthew 14:28-33

I'd like to tell you about a time that I trusted the Lord. My friends were all playing ninjas and my mom asked me to bring in six Kool-Aid drinks from the cooler for dinner. While I was getting them, I heard a terrible cry and a horrible scream! I just thought it was something little but when I came into the room, I saw my mom holding up what used to be a white, but now red blood-filled towel next to my sister's eye! She had run into the corner of the dresser, hit her cheek and cut her eyebrow open!

I started to cry because my sister is only five years old! My mom said we had to take her to the emergency room immediately! Just at that moment I remembered how Jesus held out His hand to Peter and asked him to trust in him. Then I went to my room and prayed. It was hard to keep my trust in Jesus, but I felt a little better. During dinner I kept whispering to myself these four words, "Trust in the Lord."

God brought us through this time. My sister was alright and did not have to get stitches or her head glued back together with special glue. That was a big relief!

The next time you fall, or feel glum, trust in the Lord as He is there to reach out His hand to you.

By: Anna (United States)

More from God: Proverbs 3:5

Journal Prompt: What should you do when you feel sad or fearful?

Who is Jesus?

¹⁵"But what about you?" he asked. "Who do you say I am?"

¹⁶Simon Peter answered, "You are the Messiah, the Son of the living God."

¹⁷Jesus replied, "Blessed are you, Simon son of Jonah, for this was not revealed to you by flesh and blood, but by my Father in heaven.

Matthew 16:15-17

Many people say different things about who Jesus is. Peter knew Jesus personally and walked with Him every day. It was important to Jesus to know Peter's thoughts on whom Jesus was. I think God wants all of us to think about who Jesus is and what we believe about Him. It matters what we think about God.

I believe that Jesus is God's son who came down to earth to die for us on the cross. He took all of our sins upon Himself so that we could go to heaven and live forever. I believe that He was both God and man, and that He never committed a sin, but He died for our sin. He is powerful, all knowing, wonderful, and He watches over us. He was a man that could change water into wine and calm the waves with His voice. His power was so great, he could raise people from the dead. He is always there for me whenever I need Him, especially during hard times. He created me for His glory. He is my best friend. He lives in me and wants to live in you too. Jesus is awesome and has changed my life forever.

By: Jonathan (United States)

More from God: John 11:25-27

Journal Prompt: Who do you think Jesus is? Write about your thoughts.

Bickering Brothers

¹At that time the disciples came to Jesus and asked, "Who, then, is the greatest in the kingdom of heaven?"

²He called a little child to him, and placed the child among them. ³And he said: "Truly I tell you, unless you change and become like little children, you will never enter the kingdom of heaven. ⁴Therefore, whoever takes the lowly position of this child is the greatest in the kingdom of heaven. ⁵And whoever welcomes one such child in my name welcomes me.

Matthew 18:1-5

My brothers and I used to argue a lot about things that would not matter, like whether we were the best at video games, or were the smartest in school. My parents would always tell us to stop arguing and try to help us to get along.

It made me really think about what the best way was to get along with my brothers. It seemed like they wanted to argue about everything. Matthew 18:1-6 tells about the apostles and how they were arguing to see which one of them was better. Can you imagine? Even Jesus had to deal with the same thing my parents did!

They asked Jesus which one of them was the most important in the kingdom of heaven. Jesus gives them a response they did not expect. If it were me hearing this, after trying so hard to be great in the Lord's eyes, I would be a little confused. Maybe the apostles were too. Jesus tells them to be humble and not try to lift themselves up, but instead serve each other and tell others positive things about how they are doing. So, after that, God helped me to be more encouraging and let things go when arguments started. It really did help to think about others more than myself.

By: James (United States)

More from God: 1 Peter 5:6

Journal Prompt: How can you think about others first like Jesus talked about?

Forgiveness

²¹*Then Peter came to Jesus and asked, "Lord, how many times shall I forgive my brother or sister who sins against me? Up to seven times?"*

²²*Jesus answered, "I tell you, not seven times, but seventy-seven times."*

Matthew 18:21-22

Have you ever had a time when you were mad at someone in your family? That has happened to me. My brother and I were playing with one of my toys and he broke it!

I was so mad! It was not on purpose, but I still could not forgive him! Matthew 18:21-22 says that Peter asked Jesus how many times he should forgive, and Jesus told him not 7 times, but 70 times 7!

That is a lot considering I was having a hard time

forgiving even once! Sc, I decided to forgive my brother and we played and had fun the rest of the day.

If you ever think you cannot forgive someone, pray, and ask God for help. On our own it is impossible to forgive. God helps us to do the right thing and then we can have harmony with others again like I did with my brother. It sure feels good to forgive!

By: Kenzie (United States)

More from God: Psalm 103:42

Journal Prompt: Who do you need to forgive? What will you do?

God Knows Best

²¹Jesus replied, "Truly I tell you, if you have faith and do not doubt, not only can you do what was done to the fig tree, but also you can say to this mountain, 'Go, throw yourself into the sea,' and it will be done. ²²If you believe, you will receive whatever you ask for in prayer."

Matthew 21:18-22

Have you ever prayed and God answered in a different way than what you were hoping for? I have. When I was six my mama told me she was pregnant. I was really hoping for a sister because I already had two brothers and I've always hoped for a sister. I asked and prayed to God a lot and thought that God would definitely answer my prayer.

The day we were going to find out if the baby was a boy or a girl, we went to the mountains. My dad had a confetti cannon that had powder in it and he counted down and then powder shot out.

The powder was blue. The baby was a boy. Seeing the blue powder made me feel like God did not listen to my prayers. I cried and was kind of mad and sad at the same time.

The night my baby brother was born, my mama had him at home and I got to be there to see him be born. Right after he was born, I got to hold him and cut his umbilical cord. That was special. Now Louis is a one-year-old and he is the best. I am so glad that God gave me him. God knew just what I needed.

By: Harper (United States)

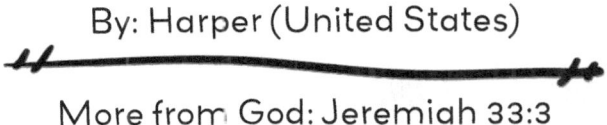

More from God: Jeremiah 33:3

Journal Prompt: Write about a time when God answered your prayers in a way that was different than you were expecting.

The On and Off Switch

Love your neighbor as yourself.

Matthew 22:39

Loving your neighbor as yourself as God tells us can be difficult. Sometimes you really don't feel like listening to what God tells you to do.

One time we were going to do a ministry project with my classmates. We were going to an elderly lady's house that lived by the school so we could work in her yard. At first, I was all happy and stuff like that, but then, I started to think about doing other things.I thought it would be more fun to do things like curling my hair, painting my fingernails, and baking cakes. I wanted to do all of that the exact day we were going to help the elderly neighbor.

I was kind of all bummed out. But finally, I thought of all the good things about visiting her, like, seeing my friends, getting to water and plant some flowers, and spending time with our kind elderly friend. So, I finally agreed with myself that I was doing this for the love of the Lord and for the neighbor. It was God calling me to do this and I needed to obey with a happy heart. I chose to love her as I would love myself.

We all went to her house and watered her flowers, had tea, and petted her cats, but most of all, just made her feel special. That is how I want to feel, so it was good that I loved her in the same way I would want to be treated myself.

By: Mary (United States)

More from God: Matthew 22:37-38

Journal Prompt: Even though it is hard sometimes, how could you love a neighbor as yourself?

Not Knowing

^{34}"Then the King will say to those on his right, 'Come, you who are blessed by my Father; take your inheritance, the kingdom prepared for you since the creation of the world. ^{35}For I was hungry and you gave me something to eat, I was thirsty and you gave me something to drink, I was a stranger and you invited me in, ^{36}I needed clothes and you clothed me, I was sick and you looked after me, I was in prison and you came to visit me.'

Matthew 25:34-36

Have you ever done something to someone without knowing what's going on in their life, and then felt bad about it? Well, I have. Once there was a new kid in my class. It seemed nobody liked him. Nobody sat with him at lunch or played with him. It seemed no one cared. Even when he dropped his pencil and he asked if someone could pick it up, everyone would just ignore him.

It kind of made me mad, but I still didn't want to be friends with him because my friends would just make fun of me because of it. He didn't deserve this.

But then one day, we were having our daily prayer time before lunch. The teacher called on him to pray. He told us about how he moved last month from Antarctica and in the same month his dad died from a disease.

It made me think of Matthew 25:34-40. I started thinking about looking at people differently. When someone is in need, I decided to look at them like I am looking at Jesus. Now I think about Jesus when I wonder what to do, and I take action like it is Jesus I am helping. It is important to help those who are unloved even when I don't understand because our attitude for the needy is like our attitude toward Jesus.

By: Hope (United States)

More from God: Matthew 5:9

Journal Prompt: Who is it you need to see through the eyes of Jesus today? What can you do to show them love like you would to Jesus?

Me? Unthankful?

²⁶While they were eating, Jesus took bread, and when he had given thanks, he broke it and gave it to his disciples, saying, "Take and eat; this is my body."

Matthew 26:26

I used to think being thankful was highly overrated. I guess you could say that I was an unthankful person. When my cousin would come over, I would want to have the cool phone she had, and things like that. It would make me unthankful for what I had because I wanted what she had.

Jesus modeled giving thanks to God in Matthew 26:26. Also, 1 Thessalonians 5:18 teaches us to be thankful in all circumstances. I read these Scriptures and prayed.

Later, some sad things happened to my cousin's family. I was really scared that I might not see my cousin again. It made me think about how God wants me to give thanks to

Him for what I have, whether it is family, friends, things, or His grace and faithfulness.

I have become much more thankful for my cousin and thankful for all God has given me. Being thankful brings peace and a joyful heart. People who are thankful are happy people. God can help you to be a thankful person just like He did for me.

By: Mariel (United States)

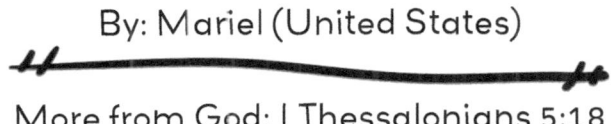

More from God: I Thessalonians 5:18

Journal Prompt: Write down things you can thank God for and think about those things as you go through your day today.

I Want That

And when Jesus had cried out again in a loud voice, he gave up his spirit.

Matthew 27:50

Have you ever felt like you never get what you want? If you have thought that, I want you to take a minute and ponder about how Jesus felt. When the Scripture says that God, "yielded up His spirit," I think it means that He gave up everything for us to put God and His will first.

That is a lot to give up! Compare your life to His life. He had to be crucified! He could have stopped that at any time because He was God. Can you imagine that level of giving up what you want? Sometimes I want life to be easy. I want to get things for myself and am mad when I can't get what I want, like a toy or something. God knew that we all were going to sin. He needed to be the only one that was perfect, as He was the perfect sacrifice for our sin. When you think about it, Jesus gave up His will for God's perfect will, which shows His great mercy and love.

I am thankful Jesus died for you and me and did not think about Himself. It makes me want to think about His will for my life and not what I want. It compels me to follow Him whole-heartedly.

By: Mary (United States)

More from God: Matthew 27:11-14

Journal Prompt: How can giving up what you want help others to see Jesus?

Spread the Word

Therefore go and make disciples of all nations, baptizing them in the name of the Father and of the Son and of the Holy Spirit

Matthew 28:19

Have you ever been on a mission trip to spread the word of God? Well, you don't always have to go someplace far away to tell others about Jesus. You can easily spread God's Word where you live. You could even spread it on public transportation, like the bus. This is something I did with some friends.

First, we put together goodie bags to hand out to the people riding the bus. These bags had candies and practical items, but the most important thing included was a Bible. When we asked people on the bus if they wanted a bag, some said, "No," but that's okay. We tried to get to know them anyway. We found that sitting at the front of the bus was better because people were happy to talk with us and others around them. When receiving the bags, some people were thankful and some did not say anything. But we were excited to share what we had and brighten someone's day. We even made special bags for the kids who rode the bus. It was fun making them smile.

It may seem a little weird, but it is one way to meet people and spread the Gospel as well as show kindness to someone who may be having a bad day. In my experience, I try and think of a Bible verse in my mind that I have memorized to be ready to share if needed. Then I am fully equipped with God's Word, a smile, and a small gift bag to make a difference in someone's life.

Whether riding a bus, going to a soccer game, being at school, or playing with a neighbor, you can always look for opportunities to encourage others with God's Word and be a missionary right where you live!

By: Mary (United States)

More from God: Hebrews 10:24-25

Journal Prompt: Can you think of a way to encourage others from God's Word today?

Saying Goodbye is Hard

16 Then the eleven disciples went to Galilee, to the mountain where Jesus had told them to go. 17 When they saw him, they worshiped him; but some doubted. 18 Then Jesus came to them and said, "All authority in heaven and on earth has been given to me. 19 Therefore go and make disciples of all nations, baptizing them in the name of the Father and of the Son and of the Holy Spirit, 20 and teaching them to obey everything I have commanded you. And surely I am with you always, to the very end of the age."

Matthew 28:16-20

Waving goodbye to my dad when he was leaving for a trip was hard. I was really sad, and scared, but God helped me. Dad was gone a long time and I had to be patient. I really missed my dad when he was gone. My dad gave me instructions on how to behave while he was away. I tried to be good for my mom and do what I knew was right. When my dad returned, I was so happy to see him!

When Jesus left earth, He commanded His disciples to trust Him and and spread the good news to every nation in the world. I am sure they were scared. They had to trust and be patient that they would see Him again in heaven someday. They went ahead and did as He commanded them. I bet it was a great, happy reunion when they were able to be reunited with Him again!

By: Cameron (United States)

More from God: John 16:7

Journal Prompt: What things does Jesus want you to be doing until you see Him in heaven someday?

Mark

Part Two:
Background to Mark

Mark, the Jew, saw Jesus serving others, and told the good news.

The second Gospel, written by Mark, shows Jesus as a servant to all. He even suffered to die as the ultimate act of serving those He loves! Mark writes a lot of the same stories as Matthew, but usually tells the stories in a shorter, more concise way. Mark seems to portray Jesus' deep love for others and His humble attitude to serve and love those who are the less fortunate. Reading these devotions from the book of Mark, you will read how kids' lives are changed because of Christ's servanthood example, as these children are willing to do what God asks and serve Him just like Mark did.

Cog Train Faith

¹The beginning of the good news about Jesus the Messiah, the Son of God, ²as it is written in Isaiah the prophet:

"I will send my messenger ahead of you, who will prepare your way"— ³"a voice of one calling in the wilderness, 'Prepare the way for the Lord, make straight paths for him.'"

Mark 1:1-3

Have you ever been afraid of being a messenger of Christ to people? Isaiah was a messenger. In the book of Mark, it records how he prophesied about John the Baptist being a messenger to tell others about Jesus. To be honest, that could be a little nerve-racking. I wonder if they ever felt that way.

God called me to do this very thing. It all started one day when I was on the Cog Railway for a field trip for school to the top of Pike's Peak in Colorado. When I got on, I was sitting across from these people. I knew they were from another country because they were speaking another language. I wasn't sure if these people had heard about Jesus.

On the way up on the train, I was very quiet and kind of shy, but as we walked around the top of Pike's Peak, God prompted me to have other plans. Right before we went down, I realized that someone brought a Bible with us. Thinking about that inspired me to make a change. So, I took the Bible in my hand, and I knew what God wanted me to do.

I felt scared, but trusted God to give me strength. Do you know what happened? I talked to them. I told them the story of Jesus, and about Noah, and many others. It was fun sharing God's Word with them, and they were interested to hear about it. In the end, I gave them the Bible and they thanked me.

To this day, I know it was God who gave me strength. God helped me to share His Word with others. Just as He helped me, He can help you do anything He calls you to do. God will give you strength to be His messenger.

By: Luke (United States)

More from God: Mark 1:4-8

Journal Prompt: If you had an opportunity to share God's Word, what might you say?

I'm Sorry

"The time has come," he said. "The kingdom of God has come near. Repent and believe the good news!"

Mark 1:15

Repenting means to be sorry for what you have done and change your ways. That is hard to do. One time I was reading, and my sister came up to me. She just started to call me names like baby, brat, and stuff like that! Has that ever happened to you?

When she called me names, I thought of not only this verse from Mark, but also Psalm 3:8, "From the Lord comes deliverance. May your blessing be on your people." So, later that night I walked up to her and told her that I liked her shirt, and that I wanted to do the dishes for her. (By the way, doing the dishes is my least favorite chore.)

The next day, my sister felt bad for what she said, and came up to me and said, "Sorry for calling you names." I told her that I would forgive her. We forgave each other and God delivered us from conflict, just like His Word says. We both chose to repent and believe that God would take care of it for us, because He forgives us when we do wrong. That IS good news!

By: Kiersten (United States)

More from God: 1 John 1:9

Journal Prompt: How can you work it out when you and your sibling do not get along with each other?

Come Follow Me

16As Jesus walked beside the Sea of Galilee, he saw Simon and his brother Andrew casting a net into the lake, for they were fishermen. 17"Come, follow me," Jesus said, "and I will send you out to fish for people." 18At once they left their nets and followed him.

Mark 1:16-18

"Mom, did people in Bible times go to school?" asked José Strauss.

"Actually, yes," said his mom. "They would memorize Scripture, and if they were the best, a Rabbi or teacher would say, 'Come follow me'. Then the student would follow that Rabbi everywhere learning all he could learn."

José asked, "What happened to the kids who weren't the best?

"Well, they would do whatever their fathers did. Mainly

fishing," said Mom. "So the disciples of Jesus were not the best in the class?" asked José.

"Maybe not according to the standards most people may have had, but Jesus thought differently. Jesus was a Rabbi or teacher to the disciples." said Mom.

"What does fishers of men mean?" asked José.

"It just means that you teach other people about Christ and draw them into having a relationship with Jesus. We all should be fishers of men."

"Maybe if God can use the disciples who may have not been considered the best in school, He can use me to teach others about Jesus too, "Jose replied.

"I'm sure God will do that," his mother said with a smile. "And don't ever forget," his mother continued, "Jesus chose you!"

By: Cy (United States)

More from God: Mark 1:19-20

Journal Prompt: Write about the type of people Jesus chooses to complete His work.

Help!

³⁵That day when evening came, he said to
his disciples, "Let us go over to the other side."
³⁶Leaving the crowd behind, they took him along,
just as he was, in the boat. There were also
other boats with him. ³⁷A furious squall came
up, and the waves broke over the boat, so that it
was nearly swamped. ³⁸Jesus was in the stern,
sleeping on a cushion. The disciples woke him
and said to him, "Teacher, don't you care if we
drown?"

³⁹He got up, rebuked the wind and said to the
waves, "Quiet! Be still!" Then the wind died down
and it was completely calm.

⁴⁰He said to his disciples, "Why are you so
afraid? Do you still have no faith?"

⁴¹They were terrified and asked each other, "Who
is this? Even the wind and the waves obey him!"

Mark 4:35-41

The disciples must have been afraid in that boat; I had that same feeling once. It all started on a Friday. My dad took his motorcycle for a ride. I was playing with my friend Katie. We were really hoping for a sleepover. Then, suddenly, my mom got a call. She got someone to watch us because she had to rush over to the hospital! There we were, left behind and full of worry! Can you guess what happened? My dad had gotten in a motorcycle accident! Things seemed to be spinning out of control! I felt afraid. Jesus calmed my heart like He calmed the storm. I found my dad had broken his arm but was going to be fine. Jesus is powerful. He can do anything. He calms us down through whatever storm or fear is going on in our lives when we trust Him.

By: Faith (United States)

More from God: Hebrews 13:6

Journal Prompt: How has Jesus helped you to overcome your fears?

Zip Lining

He said to his disciples, "Why are you so afraid? Do you still have no faith?"

Mark 4:40

When was the last time you really felt afraid? One summer, my family and I went on a field trip to Eagle Lake Camp in Colorado. I was amazed at all the beautiful scenery! I saw God in that place everywhere I looked! It was so evident to me that He made it. When we got to the lake, I saw a zip line hanging over the lake. It looked rather fun. Later, we hiked up to the top where the zip line began. It was really high and fear started to fill my entire body! I was very worried. The counselors encouraged me to try. Once I stepped off and flew down that zip line over the lake, it was the most fun I ever had in my life! My fear turned to complete joy!

Just as it took faith to step out on that zip line, so it takes faith to trust God to complete what He asks us to do. Maybe God wants us to talk to a neighbor about Him or give up something we have in order to help a needy person. Sometimes He asks us to do things that are very uncomfortable for us and fear takes over. We need to step out in faith, not be afraid, and follow God's word to do what He asks us to do. Doing this is the greatest adventure we could have. Even more adventurous than zip lining!

By: Baylee (United States)

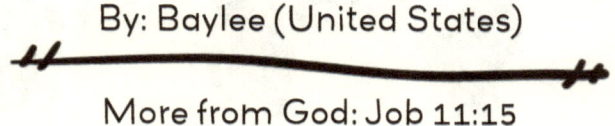

More from God: Job 11:15

Journal Prompt: Think about something difficult God has asked you to do that may bring you anxious thoughts. Write a prayer asking God to give you faith in Him to accomplish it.

Waldo Canyon Fire

⁴⁷Later that night, the boat was in the middle of the lake, and he was alone on land. ⁴⁸He saw the disciples straining at the oars, because the wind was against them. Shortly before dawn he went out to them, walking on the lake. He was about to pass by them, ⁴⁹but when they saw him walking on the lake, they thought he was a ghost. They cried out, ⁵⁰because they all saw him and were terrified.

Immediately he spoke to them and said, "Take courage! It is I. Don't be afraid." ⁵¹Then he climbed into the boat with them, and the wind died down. They were completely amazed, ⁵²for they had not understood about the loaves; their hearts were hardened.

Mark 6:47-52

Have you ever been afraid of a natural disaster? One

morning in late June, I woke up early. It was a normal day like any other day with my chores to do. After chores, my sister and I jumped on our trampoline. All of a sudden, we realized it smelled like smoke. We came to find out there was a fire in Waldo Canyon, not too far from our house! At first it didn't seem threatening or concerning to me, so we went about the day doing other things. Our cousins were in town, so we went out to lunch with them. They came home to hang out with us for awhile.

Later we went into our sun room and I looked out the window. There was a big red blob storming down the mountain right toward our house! It was a fire! I was scared! I was running all over the place. I felt like everything was falling apart! In all the commotion there was one thing I forgot to do! Obey God! God tells us over and over again in the Bible not to be afraid. I learned that just because things look bad, there is no excuse to be afraid.

I took my eyes off Jesus and panicked. It made me think about the disciples in the boat in the middle of the windstorm. Jesus told them not to be afraid and got in the boat with them. At that point, I knew Jesus was with me and I should not be afraid. God protected my family from the fire, and I am thankful for the way He is always with me in the storms of life.

By: Luke (United States)

More from God: Genesis 26:24

Journal Prompt: Think about a time when something in nature such as lightning, flood, fire, hail, earthquake or hurricane caused you to be fearful. What did you do?

Do Not Worry

...Immediately he spoke to them and said, "Take courage! It is I. Don't be afraid."

Mark 6:50

What can help you not to worry or be fearful?

One morning I arrived at school like any other day. I noticed I forgot my backpack and right away became worried. This may seem like a small thing to you, but it was Friday, and I had a lot of tests, and my homework was in my backpack! My grades would really suffer if I did not turn in the work.

When I walked into the auditorium where the students wait for their teachers, I was very nervous. My stomach was all in knots!

Little did I know that my dad was taking care of me. He was bringing my backpack to school and our principal brought it into my classroom for me. Boy, was I relieved!

I realized that worrying and being fearful is a sin and the Lord does not want me to do this. Just like my dad was looking out for me, my Heavenly Father, Jesus, always looks out for me too.

Jesus goes before all of us, behind us, and all around us to watch over and help us. He helps us in big and small ways daily. If we just take the time to realize how He works and intervenes, we will daily see His love and protection.

By: Nash (United States)

More from God: Isaiah 26:3

Journal Prompt: How have you seen God's love and protection?

No Food - God Delivers

53 When they had crossed over, they landed at Gennesaret and anchored there. 54 As soon as they got out of the boat, people recognized Jesus. 55 They ran throughout that whole region and carried the sick on mats to wherever they heard he was. 56 And wherever he went—into villages, towns or countryside—they placed the sick in the marketplaces. They begged him to let them touch even the edge of his cloak, and all who touched it were healed.

Mark 6:53-56

The Gospel of Mark records how Jesus delivered people from all kinds of things. People came to Him all the time to be delivered from sickness, enemies, demons, hunger, and fear. People just wanted to get to Jesus because they knew He had the power to do anything! He had the power then, and He still has the power today to do the same.

One day we had no food in my house. My family had

no money. None. My dad was out of work. My mother was feeling bad for us kids with nothing to eat. We were lying there trying to go to sleep, but it was hard with empty stomachs. Suddenly, we heard a knock on the door! It was our neighbor who came to give us some flour and vegetables. We then rejoiced and thanked God for delivering us from hunger! God cares about us. Every good thing comes from God. Just as God helped people in the Bible with many needs, so He wants to help people today.

By: Lucy (Kenya)

More from God: Psalm 34:17

Journal Prompt: Write a note to God thanking Him for a way He has delivered you.

Hypocrisy

⁶He replied, "Isaiah was right when he prophesied about you hypocrites; as it is written:

"'These people honor me with their lips, but their hearts are far from me. ⁷They worship me in vain; their teachings are merely human rules.' ⁸You have let go of the commands of God and are holding on to human traditions."

Mark 7:6-8

As a missionary kid overseas in Cambodia, most of the people I come into contact with are either devout Christians or the total opposite, which over there is called, "pagans." It wasn't until I came to the U.S. that I noticed a strange behavior that the Bible rebukes. Starting school in the States was a little different for me. I began a quest to look for kids who either said they were Christians or went to a church youth group because I wanted some good friends. However, many of the kids I did find who said they were Christians didn't act like the Christians they were claiming to be. It was strange to hear them listening to bad music or have dishonoring language. Many didn't treat others respectfully. They hung around questionable company. I wondered if this is what the word hypocrisy means.

What does the Bible say about hypocrites? The Bible makes it very clear about what a hypocrite is-people who say they love God yet don't live it out. Hypocrisy is one of my least favorite words. It's a word that describes a deception of character. Hypocrites not only give themselves a bad reputation, but also can taint the reputation of others who are perhaps more sincere.

These kids I observed were listening to the wrong things and saying the wrong words, when the Bible tells us clearly to listen closely to His Word and keep them in our hearts and to keep corrupt words from our lips (Proverbs 4:20-25). They didn't give teachers and other adults the respect they were due. The Bible instructs us to give respect to those in authority (Malachi 1:6). They associated themselves with bad company, which the Bible warns against (1 Corinthians 15:33). It made me sad. I really noticed the hypocrisy in the kids my age. So as a fellow young Christian, I want to encourage all of you to read this, to set an example for your peers and for those younger and older than you (1Timothy 4:12). Please take encouragement from this and know that someone around the world (in Cambodia) is praying for you. God Bless and Shalom.

By: Paul (Cambodia)

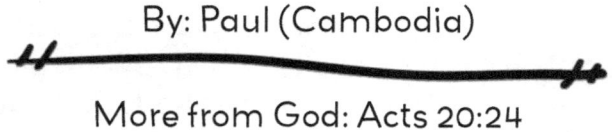

More from God: Acts 20:24

Journal Prompt: What is a hypocrite? Have you ever seen this in your own life?

Life's Not Perfect

Then he called the crowd to him along with his disciples and said: "Whoever wants to be my disciple must deny themselves and take up their cross and follow me.

Mark 8:34

Before I knew God, when I went to church, I didn't really understand what it meant. Then at a young age, I decided to follow God as my Savior. I realized Jesus died for my sins and I could be forgiven and trust Him with my life. After that, I really knew what it meant to deny myself, put God first, and follow Jesus, even at a young age. I understood. To this day I am glad He is my Savior because without Him I wouldn't be able to go to heaven, for Romans 6:23 says, "For the wages of sin is death, but the free gift of God is eternal life." Being one of His disciples has changed my life.

Even as a follower of Christ, life is still not perfect. Bad things happen sometimes even in families. It was tough because 3-5 months after I accepted Jesus as my

Savior, my parents went through a divorce. But I did not go through it alone. God was helping me along the way. I would cry at night sometimes, but I was always comforted when I thought about how God was taking care of me and loving me. Jesus has walked with me every step of the way and will continue to do so. I am His disciple and will continue to follow Him as He guides and directs.

By: Justin (United States)

More from God: Mark 2:17

Journal Prompt: How has Jesus walked with you during a hard time?

Little Steps With a Big God

"'If you can'?" said Jesus. "Everything is possible for one who believes."

Mark 9:23

I thought it was impossible for my friend named Ismelin to ever be able to walk. She had problems with her bones and no one to help. The surgeries she needed cost a lot of money. She asked God for a miracle. God sent some people to help raise money so she could have surgeries to fix her problem.

God did the impossible! Ismelin is now taking little steps with crutches! It is so good to see her walking! God is working to heal her body and help her get stronger daily.

God helps you during bad and good times. When you believe in God, He always shows Himself to you in amazing ways. You can recognize and see Him working each day.

Taking the time to stop and think about the impossible situations that God is working will help your faith to grow little steps at a time, just like my friend. I want to believe God more to help me with the impossible things. How about you?

By: Pricila (Dominican Republic)

More from God: Job 26:14

Journal Prompt: Look around at what God is doing today. Why is it important to know that everything is possible with God?

For more information on this ministry go to:

https://visiontrust.org/

I Thought She Liked Me!

"Why do you call me good?" Jesus answered. "No one is good—except God alone.

Mark 10:18

Have you ever thought that someone liked you, but then you find out they don't just because you did one little teeny, tiny thing?

There was this girl in my class and we used to be really good friends. We would play on the swings, and the shaped twisty things. But then one day we were playing Capture the Flag in P.E. class, and we were on opposite teams. I was playing defense, and she was running to our circle to get the flag. The object of the game is to get the other team's flag and bring it to your own team's circle without getting tagged. Our team thought it was unfair that their team would run in our circle, stay there, and wait for us to bring our flag there, then just grab it and take off to their side and put it in their circle! We talked to our P.E.

teacher about it and he thought it was fair. So, we started a new game. Sure enough, the same thing happened again. I got a flag that a girl from our team took from their circle, and I just stood there and held it! (This did not go over well.) My friend was surprisingly yelling at me as loud as she could to put it in the circle. I said, "No, because it's not fair!" This whole thing made me mad, and she was mad at me too. This was just a game; why was she so mad at me?

After talking to both of my BFF's, I asked if one of them would talk to her. After thinking about it, I should have gone and talked to her myself because what she told them really hurt me. Even though I was mad, it didn't seem like that big of a deal to dislike a person because of this little thing.

This whole thing made me think about people. People seem to disappoint us at times. I probably disappointed her just like she disappointed me. No one is good all the time. Jesus said that the only one who is always good is God. We can trust in Him to be our best friend and love us the way we are. Whether we act right, or do hurtful things, God is always there for us.

Sometimes, life is not fair, and we all say and do hurtful things. When this happens, talk to God about it and know He is good all the time. Because He is good, He can help us to do good to those who have hurt us or when we hurt others and things seem unfair.

By: Hope (United States)

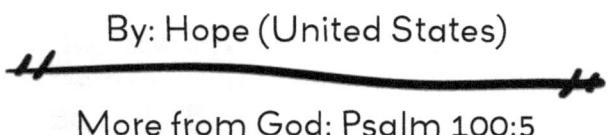

More from God: Psalm 100:5

Journal Prompt: How can you relate my story to something that happened to you?

Hugs

13 People were bringing little children to Jesus for him to place his hands on them, but the disciples rebuked them... 16And he took the children in his arms, placed his hands on them and blessed them.

Mark 10:13,16

Have you ever needed a hug? Hugs come in all different ways. They don't cost anything but are worth a lot. Sometimes a hug can be like a little tap on the back. Other times it can be an arm around the shoulders. Our family gives group hugs. At times it is like an octopus wrapping all around you!

When I hug my grandma she smiles and gives me an extra big hug back! Then Grandpa joins in too! My sister is fun to hug as she is little. I have to be careful not to hug her too tight. Hugs are the best. It makes me feel cared for and cheers me up if I am feeling upset.

When someone you love gives you a hug it really makes

you feel blessed. I'm sure those children coming to Jesus felt so loved as he took them in his arms. It's amazing to think about the God of the universe taking little kids in His arms and showing them value and blessing them with hugs! He loves kids of all ages and enjoys blessing us as a good father does!

Inspired by Wyatt (United States)

More from God: Mark 10:14-15

Journal Prompt: Name a time you felt blessed by someone who gave you a hug like Jesus did for the children. Why should you be willing to do this for others also?

Serve it Up

For even the Son of Man did not come to be served, but to serve, and to give his life as a ransom for many.

Mark 10:45

One time my class went to the Rescue Mission. This is a place for people to come who need help. We wanted to brighten their day and show them God's love. We sang Christmas carols and gave the children gifts.

It felt really good to do things for others who have less than we do. Serving others is a cool thing to do. Thinking about others brought me much joy.

There are many ways to serve others. You could rake someone's lawn, shovel a walk, make a gift for someone, or help others as we did. Jesus was a good example of this as He left His place in heaven to come and serve us!

Jesus walked around feeding others, healing others,

caring for others, and giving all He had for others. He loved us so much! He served us in the ultimate way by giving His life for us! Serving others is the least I can do to show thankfulness for all He has done for me.

By: Jennifer (United States)

More from God: 1 Peter 4:10

Journal Prompt: Can you give an example of how Jesus served others? How can you serve others?

Moving

Therefore I tell you, whatever you ask for in prayer, believe that you have received it, and it will be yours.

Mark 11:24

Did you ever have to move? Once, right after school was out for the year, my dad called a family meeting. Usually family meetings are fun, but this one I did not like. My dad said that we were moving to a new city.

I got really upset. My mom assured us that everything will be alright. (She always does that.) I was worried about moving and making new friends. I prayed and asked God to help me be brave.

When we got to our new state, we looked for schools. My mom called a few moms at my new school, and they arranged play time with me and their kids. After meeting the boys, we started to become friends. When I got home that night I slept great! I was so stressed out about moving and making new friends, but God took care of everything!

I've learned to trust God more! Psalm 4:1 says "Answer me when I call to you, O my righteous God. Give me relief from my distress; be merciful to me and hear my prayer." I asked God for help, and He answered. He will answer you too.

By: Benjamin (United States)

More from God: Mark 5:21-24

For more information on this school go to:

https://www.cscslions.org/

Luke

Part 3:
Background to Luke

Luke was a doctor and a friend of Paul. Together they did ministry and shared the Gospel to others. When Luke, wrote about Jesus' healings, he knew firsthand the true miracle it was each time Jesus touched someone. Luke liked to write with lots of details, which helps the reader to know more of the history behind what was happening. Luke knew how to speak the truth to others. His whole mission was to tell sinners of Jesus' saving grace and sacrifice of dying on the cross. He captured the true story for the world to know. The devotions in Luke will help you understand God's Word is truth to give you inspiration.

Why, God?

For no word from God will ever fail.

Luke 1:37

Do you ever sit in class on the last day of school and think about all the fun you are going to have that summer? I had some great plans! I planned to swim a lot, compete in volleyball tournaments with my friends, take a vacation with my family, have sleepovers, and have outdoor movie nights! I thought about my to-do list and getting started on it right away. I never could have imagined the summer God had planned.

I had several bad headaches during the school year, which had gotten worse. The doctors found the reason for my headaches. I had a brain tumor. CANCER was not on my summer to-do list!

Having cancer makes me mad. I get mad when it is time to leave for my chemotherapy because I don't want to get in the car or be in the hospital every day.

I'm scared lying on the table for radiation. It's cold and I'm in the room all alone. I also was scared when my hair started falling out because I liked having my long hair. I cried when I shaved my hair because my scalp hurt. I don't like being nauseous and tired all the time. I miss seeing things all around me. I miss vivid colors and brightness. I wish I could hear without my ears ringing all the time. I get mad when I think about missing my summer fun. I just miss me and want to feel better.

Luke 1:37 says, "Nothing is impossible with God." This verse reminds me that even though I have days where I feel good and a little bit like my old self, and I have days where I feel grouchy and yucky and angry and mad and sad and helpless, God is always by my side. Nothing is impossible as long as He is with me. This verse tells me that God is asking me to have faith in Him that He will get me through this. I DO KNOW that my God loves me.

By: Hannah (United States)

More from God: Ephesians 3:20

Journal Prompt: Think about something that seems impossible for you to go through. Be honest with God and tell Him about it.

What is God Like?

46 And Mary said:

"My soul glorifies the Lord

47 and my spirit rejoices in God my Savior,

48 for he has been mindful

   of the humble state of his servant.

From now on all generations will call me blessed,

49 for the Mighty One has done great things for me—holy is his name.

50 His mercy extends to those who fear him,

   from generation to generation.

51 He has performed mighty deeds with his arm; he has scattered those who are proud in their inmost thoughts.

Luke 1:46-51

Mary described what God was like to her as a prayer of worship. She described Him as being mighty, merciful, and her Savior. I want to tell you what I believe God is like. I think He is huge and powerful. Even though He has so much power, God is loving and kind, and a faithful companion. I know this firsthand because when my dad was in Afghanistan, my family prayed and prayed that he would come home safely. We knew God was with my dad no matter what happened. God brought him home safely! We felt God's presence and care during this hard time. He also showed my family His power, love, and kindness.

God is also forgiving. Considering how many bad things we do, God must forgive us a trillion times a day! When we ask Him to forgive us, He wipes away our sins. It says in Isaiah 43:25 that God removes our sin and doesn't even remember it anymore!

I think of God as also being very powerful. He made us and the world easily! Even though Satan may frighten us because he is evil, we can know that he also has to bow to God. God is more powerful than Satan. God loves us so much and wants to help us make good choices. When I worship God, I picture Him as being kind, forgiving, powerful, and breathtaking! I hope you see that too!

By: Benjamin (United States)

More from God: Deuteronomy 3:24

Journal Prompt: What do you think God is like? Write a worship prayer to God.

Kindness Rocks

His mercy extends to those who fear him, from generation to generation.

Luke 1:50

God is kind and shows mercy to us. He promises to do this to those who fear him. Because God does that for us, we can show kindness to others, even when we feel bullied.

One time I was at wrestling practice and my teammate and I were messing around and having a lot of fun. But then he hurt me with his words. Then all the fun stopped and he said some really mean things to me. I tried to ignore him, but that didn't work. I told the coach and he talked to my friend. He told him if he kept doing that, he would need to sit out, so my friend went to the other side of the room and sat out. But when he came back, he just kept being mean to me. I talked to my mom about it. After that I remembered that God extends kindness to everyone, and I should too. Because of God's kindness towards me, I can be kind to others. So, I started to be nicer to my friend. He saw that kindness and started being kind back to me. It worked! Ephesians 4:32 tells us to "Be kind and compassionate to one another, forgiving one another just as Christ forgave you." This is hard to do, but God gave me the courage and it really helped.

By: Stephen (United States)

More from God: Psalm 100:5

Journal Prompt: How has being kind helped you in a situation with friends?

From Worst to Best Christmas

³And everyone went to their own town to register.

⁴So Joseph also went up from the town of Nazareth in Galilee to Judea, to Bethlehem the town of David, because he belonged to the house and line of David. ⁵He went there to register with Mary, who was pledged to be married to him and was expecting a child. ⁶While they were there, the time came for the baby to be born, ⁷and she gave birth to her firstborn, a son. She wrapped him in cloths and placed him in a manger, because there was no guest room available for them.

Luke 2:3-7

Once, it was the day before Christmas, and I could not wait. There was this dollhouse I really wanted, and I was sure I was going to get it. I had put it on wish list.

After decorating the tree, we set out some milk for Santa and went to bed. The next morning, I woke up really early and I zoomed downstairs to open my stocking. It was filled with all kinds of stuff! We started to play, and then a few minutes later my family was awake and we all opened presents! After that I realized I was missing something! The dollhouse I wanted was not there!

I started to cry. My mom explained to me that I didn't need to cry because I already had the best gift in the world. I asked, "What would be better than a dollhouse?" My mom replied, "Jesus." She then read Luke 2:3-7 to me. After that, I understood what Christmas was really about. Jesus came to earth for us and gave His life so we could live eternally with Him. After I realized how Jesus could be so much better than having a dollhouse, I stopped crying. Now whenever I am tempted to only think of myself, I think about how Jesus thought of others to give the perfect gift!

By: Maddie (United States)

More from God: 2 Corinthians 9:15

A New Bed

This will be a sign to you: You will find a baby wrapped in cloths and lying in a manger."

Luke 2:12

One night I was lying in bed thinking to myself how great it would be if I had a new bed. In the morning, I remembered that we were going to Grand Cayman after school for a vacation. After school we went to the airport. When we arrived, we checked-in to the hotel. It was around 9:00 p.m. and we were tired; so, we put all our clothes away and then when to bed.

The next morning, I asked my dad if we could drive by the poorer part of the island on the way to the beach. I noticed that a lot of kids didn't have a house. I realized that most of these kids didn't even have a bed!

I thought about Jesus that first night He was born not having a cozy bed either but sleeping in a manger. Jesus knew what those children felt like without a bed! He gave up living in heaven with all the comfortable things to come down to earth where He had to live in poor conditions many times. Jesus experienced all those hard things because He loves us so much!

It made me thankful for my nice bed at home. It made me thankful that Jesus cared enough for me to come to earth and go through hardships just like people on earth do. Because of His love for us, it makes me want to reach out to others and be more thankful for what I have.

By: Kenzie (United States)

More from God: James 1:17

Journal Prompt: Write about a time that God helped you to feel thankful.

Cleaning Time

And Jesus grew in wisdom and stature, and in favor with God and man.

Luke 2:52

Have your parents ever told you to clean when you didn't want to? I was at my house and was playing video games and my friend was playing with me. We were having so much fun. My parents had instructed me to clean my room, but of course I didn't. We just kept right on playing video games. An hour later or so, we were asked to turn off the Xbox, but again I didn't listen and played another hour. It was about two o'clock and I was still playing video games!

My mom was coming home at three o'clock, so I turned off the Xbox. I walked upstairs, but not happily. I started to clean and was done right about the time when my mom came home. I was able to play with my friend for the rest of the day. Even though it turned out alright, I should have obeyed first and then played later. Even though my attitude was bad, I have learned to listen to my parents and am growing in many ways. Jesus was perfect and gave us the example of doing the right thing. Just as Jesus grew up being wise and making good choices, He is helping me to learn that, too.

By: Stephen (United States)

More from God: Colossians 3:20

Journal Prompt: Describe a time you didn't want to listen when you were asked to do something. What better choice will you make next time?

Share the Love

Anyone who has two shirts should share with the one who has none, and anyone who has food should do the same.

Luke 3:11

I have many shoes. I wonder what it would be like to have no shoes to wear every day. I have three meals a day. What would it be like to not even know where your next meal is coming from? Imagine not having books to read or even a pencil to use to write with at school. My classroom is filled with colorful learning tools and many school supplies.

My teacher told our class about a place in the Dominican Republic where kids do not have enough food, clothes, or even supplies to go to school. Jesus tells us to share what we have with others. We decided to help. We organized a supply drive to get school supplies and not only shared the extra we had, but also got new notebooks, crayons, pencils, crafts, and binders. Since my teacher was going on a mission trip to the Dominican Republic, she could take them to give to the kids. When she brought pictures back of the happy faces showing those kids with the supplies we had sent, it made my heart so glad that we shared what we had.

Sometimes we don't realize how much God has blessed us with and forget to share that with others. Thinking about this, and doing it for others not only supports them, but blesses our life too. Jesus gives us everything we have, so we should want to share it with others.

By: An Anonymous Giver

More from God: Deuteronomy 16:17

Journal Prompt: What does this story make you think about

Shine Baby Shine

^{12}One of those days Jesus went out to a mountainside to pray, and spent the night praying to God. ^{13}When morning came, he called his disciples to him and chose twelve of them, whom he also designated apostles: ^{14}Simon (whom he named Peter), his brother Andrew, James, John, Philip, Bartholomew, ^{15}Matthew, Thomas, James son of Alphaeus, Simon who was called the Zealot, ^{16}Judas son of James, and Judas Iscariot, who became a traitor.

Luke 6:12-16

The apostles were all disciples. A disciple is a follower of God. The apostles were special disciples chosen by Jesus himself. Anyone can be a disciple. The apostles were fishermen, tax collectors, and many other things too.

God uses disciples to shine His light and show people

His love. Has God ever called you to do something a disciple would do? Once, my class went to Crossfire Ministries. This is a place where needy or homeless people go to get food and many other things to help them get by or live. I brought a football to give as a gift.

As I was standing and waiting, God called me to give my football to a lady with a little kid. After that, I felt happy that I had done something God called me to do as His disciple. I knew I'd done the right thing. God can use anyone to spread His love and light, even kids!

By: Dylan (United States)

More from God: Psalm 37:3

Journal Prompt: How can you spread God's light to others? Write down some ideas.

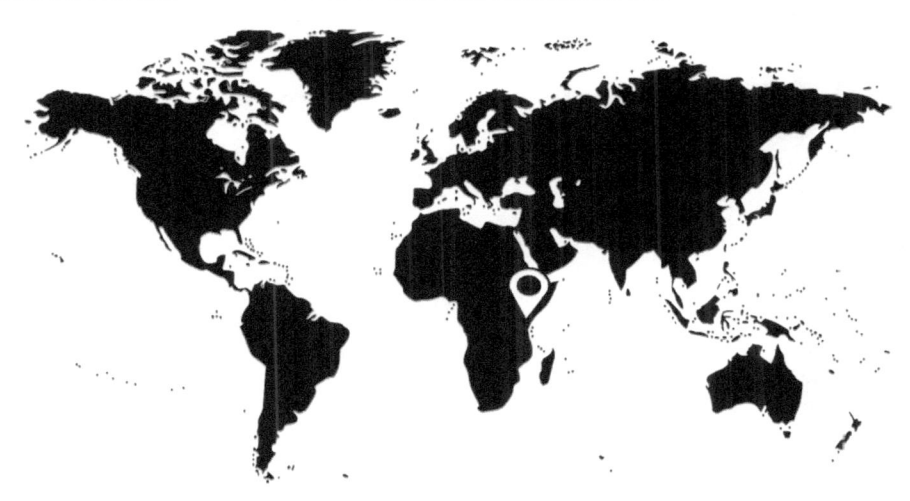

Shoes From God

Give to everyone who asks you, and if anyone takes what belongs to you, do not demand it back.

Luke 6:30

One day I was in school, and my shoes were too small and in bad condition. My family did not have the money to buy new shoes for me. My teacher really wanted me to have shoes. I went home and was praying every day that God would somehow supply me with a pair of shoes. One day when I went to school, I was so surprised. My teacher bought a pair of shoes for me! I thank God so much for her every time I pray. She gave to me and helped me because Jesus had given to her. I want to do the same for others. I am so thankful for my shoes and a caring teacher.

Inspired by Purity (Kenya)

More from God: 1 John 3:17

Journal Prompt: What can you thank God for that someone has given to you? Make a list of things you are thankful for, as everything we have ultimately comes from God.

Family Forgiveness

Do not judge, and you will not be judged. Do not condemn, and you will not be condemned. Forgive, and you will be forgiven.

Luke 6:37

Have you ever had a time when you were so mad at someone in your family? That has happened to me. My brother and I were playing with one of my toys and he broke it!

Even though it was not on purpose, I was so mad because it was one of my favorite things to play with! I felt like I could not forgive him.

Jesus tells us to forgive so we can be forgiven too. I thought about the Scripture from Luke 6:37, and about times I needed to be forgiven for things I had done. After that, I forgave my brother, and we played the rest of the day together and had a great time.

Maybe you can think of someone you need to forgive. Pray and ask God to help you. It can be hard at first, but feels so good once you have really forgiven that person. We all mess up and need forgiveness from time to time, especially brothers and sisters.

By: Gentri (United States)

More from God: Matthew 18:21

Journal Prompt: Journal about a time when it was hard for you to forgive someone. What did you do?

Cruise Into Giving

Give, and it will be given to you. A good measure, pressed down, shaken together and running over, will be poured into your lap. For with the measure you use, it will be measured to you.

Luke 6:38

One time my family and I went on a cruise. I had a lot of fun! When we got back, I realized not a lot of people can take a vacation like that. I wanted other people to be able to do something fun and special with their family too.

God gave me the idea to donate money to a "fun-func" every week. This helps provide the money a family may need to do something they normally could not do. I was thankful for the chance to do something special and I'm thankful I can help others in this way too.

God wants us to give to others. He also says in Proverbs 3:9 to "Honor the Lord with all your wealth, with the first fruits of your crops." Giving to God first is most important.

God will show you how He wants you to use what He has blessed you with to help others.

By: Caleb (United States)

More from God: 2 Corinthians 9:7

Journal Prompt: Think about how God has blessed you. Who can you share it with?

Did I Just Say That?

⁴³"No good tree bears bad fruit, nor does a bad tree bear good fruit. ⁴⁴Each tree is recognized by its own fruit. People do not pick figs from thornbushes, or grapes from briers.

Luke 6:43-44

"Did I just say that?" I thought as I sat in the principal's office. It all started at the beginning of the day. I walked in and my friend Rebecca ran up and scared me half to death!

"Why didn't you call me last night?" Rebecca said.

"I was busy," I snapped back.

"Doing what?" She replied.

Thankfully the teacher just then wanted our attention for the spelling lesson. After the spelling lesson we went to recess.

Rebecca was waiting for me at the swings. She was still bugging me about last night. I got mad and called her a name. Charlie heard me and of course told the teacher. So. . . Here we sat in the principal's office. If I could have a do-over, I would have remembered that God can give me the right words of wisdom, not words of contempt. Words matter and I can't take back what I said now. I feel bad, but I know that God will forgive me, and I will ask forgiveness from Rebecca too. When I act in a way that displeases God, others see that and start to recognize me for that. I kind of get a bad reputation, as some people would say.

I prayed for God to help me make a change. I want to be known as bearing good fruit, or a person who God uses to bless others. I do not want to be known for being in the principal's office for doing or saying the wrong thing! Next time, I will use words that build up and help others, then good things will come of it and not bad.

I learned from all this that choosing to do the right thing helps others to recognize you as someone who bears good fruit and God is glorified through that.

By: Mariah (United States)

More from God: 1 John 3:18

Journal Prompt: Would others recognize you for bearing good fruit? If not, what can you do to change it?

Tell People About Jesus

"Return home and tell how much God has done for you." So the man went away and told all over town how much Jesus had done for him.

Luke 8:39

Have you ever told someone about what God has done for you? One time I was with my friend at a park and saw people fighting and pushing people off the slide. Later, for some reason, I felt prompted to ask these kids, "Do you know Jesus?" One boy said "No." My friend and I told him how Jesus died for us and for them too. He forgave us of our sins. We told them that we believe in Jesus Christ as our Savior, and we will go to heaven to live with Him someday. The boy said, "Okay, I will tell my mom about it."

That same day at the park, God also led us to some kids who looked sad. As we played with them, we told them about Jesus and His love and peace too. God helped us to tell others what He had done for us. It is up to the Holy

Spirit to prompt them to follow God. It felt good to share God's plan and tell others about what He has done for us.

It may be at the park, at school, during soccer practice, or other times, but God will show you people who need Him. Ask God what to say and be willing to talk about what Jesus has done for you, and let God do the rest!

By: Madison (United States)

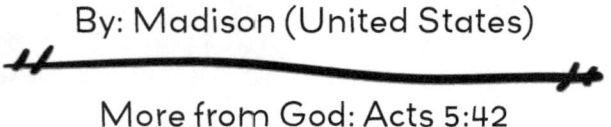

More from God: Acts 5:42

Journal Prompt: What has God done in your life or someone else's life that prompts you to talk about it to others?

Not Yet

42...As Jesus was on his way, the crowds almost crushed him. 43And a woman was there who had been subject to bleeding for twelve years, but no one could heal her. 44She came up behind him and touched the edge of his cloak, and immediately her bleeding stopped.

45"Who touched me?" Jesus asked.

When they all denied it, Peter said, "Master, the people are crowding and pressing against you."

46But Jesus said, "Someone touched me; I know that power has gone out from me."

47Then the woman, seeing that she could not go unnoticed, came trembling and fell at his feet. In the presence of all the people, she told why she had touched him and how she had been instantly healed. 48Then he said to her, "Daughter, your faith has healed you. Go in peace."

Luke 8:42- 48

This woman, who came to Jesus, had been sick for 12 years! She must have prayed often for the blessing of healing. She came to Jesus trembling and unnoticed. She probably felt invisible! Maybe she felt like God wanted her to move forward to go to Him, but she didn't think she could do it. She had waited a long time for God to answer her prayer. Yet God, in His time, saw her faith and did His work in her life.

Maybe you have also had a time in your life when God wanted you to do something, but you did not think you could do it. Maybe you have felt unnoticed also. I was not sick as this woman was, but I did want to be noticed to receive a blessing in another way.

One day, in 3rd Grade, we had to say our speech for the Speech Meet. I practiced hard and said it, but God didn't answer the way I wanted. I did not make it to the Speech Meet finals. Then later, I tried to make the Spelling Bee, but went unnoticed. Soon came the Sword Drill Competition. This is an event in which the teacher gives a Scripture reference from God's Word, and we see who can find it the quickest. I practiced and found the key to finding verses quickly. It was to read my Bible every day. When I spent time in God's Word my faith grew and so did my Sword Drill skills! God blessed me by answering my prayer! Just when I didn't think I could do it, He allowed me to do my best in the competition. I went in peace knowing it was all about God and the faith He gave to me, not about myself. He was glorified and my faith grew when He blessed me and answered my prayer.

I'm thankful God blessed the woman and she went in peace. God touches us also in personal ways so He can receive the praise and we feel blessed to see Him working.

By: Amanda (United States)

More from God: Galatians 1:3

Journal Prompt: What can you give God praise for today?

A True Foster Story

Hearing this, Jesus said to Jairus, "Don't be afraid; just believe, and she will be healed."

Luke 8:50

Jairus, in this Scripture, was really afraid because he thought his daughter had died. There are times in our lives when we are really afraid too. I have had a past of living in fear. I'm not just talking about being afraid of the dark. When I was young, I was really scared because I had a rough family life. Things were very difficult for me. I would go back and forth from one relative to another. I felt alone. It was very stressful. It never occurred to me to go to Jesus for help.

Because of some hard circumstances, I was taken from my home and placed in a foster home. This is a home where kids go when their parents can't care for them. I was afraid, but when I met my foster mom, she was really nice. I am now adopted. Later, something happened to me that changed my life. I accepted Jesus as my Savior, and now I know that Jesus is always with me, through good times and bad. I realize there is no need to be afraid because God is right by me. I do not have to live in fear anymore. I believed and Jesus healed my heart.

No matter what, God can take care of you just as He has taken care of me. I was not only adopted into a foster family, but I was also adopted into God's family. Living with God as my heavenly Father, I do not have to live in fear anymore, but in hope for a bright future.

By: Genessa (United States)

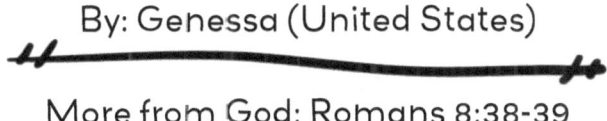

More from God: Romans 8:38-39

Journal Prompt: God is always with you no matter what happens in life. Try to memorize Romans 8:38-39 as you write it.

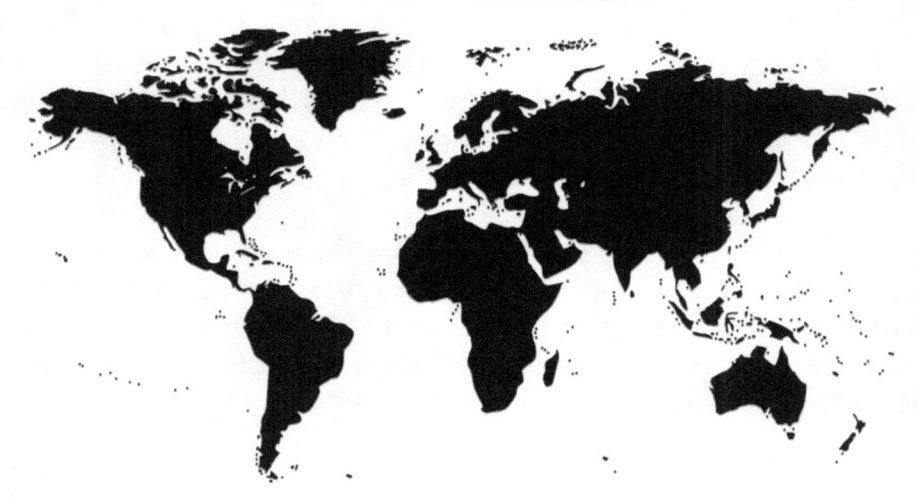

Just Go

¹When Jesus had called the Twelve together, he gave them power and authority to drive out all demons and to cure diseases, ²and he sent them out to proclaim the kingdom of God and to heal the sick. ³He told them: "Take nothing for the journey—no staff, no bag, no bread, no money, no extra shirt. ⁴Whatever house you enter, stay there until you leave that town. ⁵If people do not welcome you, leave their town and shake the dust off your feet as a testimony against them." ⁶So they set out and went from village to village, proclaiming the good news and healing people everywhere.

Luke 9:1-6

Have you ever gone to proclaim the good news to people like the disciples did? When I was younger, my family went on a mission trip to Mexico. I felt like the disciples going out to tell people the good news of Jesus. We went to different places and helped orphans, fed hungry people, and prayed for those who were sick. I remember one mom who had a little boy with an eye infection. She did not have the money to take her son to a doctor and the infection got worse and went into both eyes, until the little boy became blind! The mom was so sad. We prayed for the little boy and the mom. I also remember walking down dusty dirt roads with many happy children scampering behind us. We gladly played soccer with them in the streets and gave them piggyback rides. Many times, I wasn't sure about what to say or how to say it because I do not know Spanish as well as I should, but God gave me the words and actions to let them know about His love. It was cool to go somewhere different, and I learned a lot about who God is and how He can work through me to love others.

I'm sure it wasn't easy for the disciples to go to new places, but God was with them every step of the way, just like He was with me. Going to different places to tell people about Jesus and share His love is important. It not only helps others but will change your life too.

By: A Young Missionary

More from God: Mark 6:15

Journal Prompt: Where would you choose to go and tell someone about Jesus?

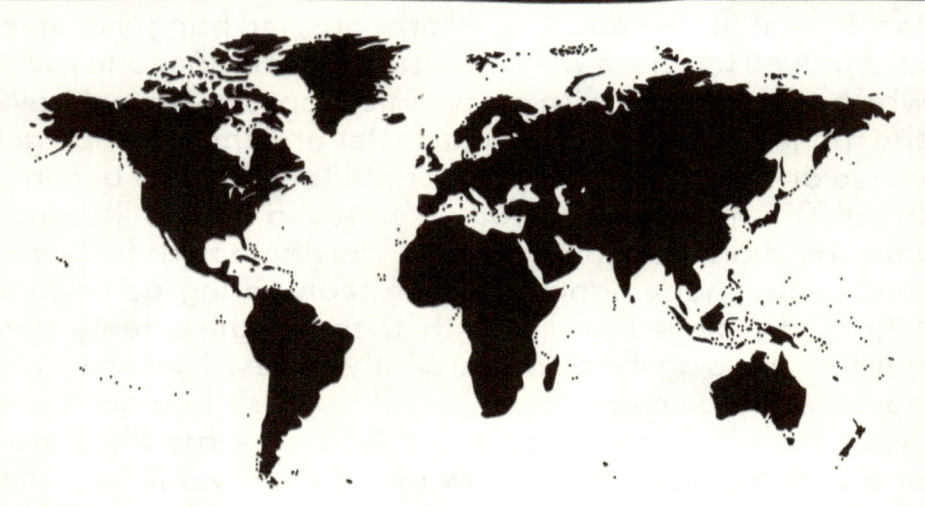

Pass the Jam

¹²*Late in the afternoon the Twelve came to him and said, "Send the crowd away so they can go to the surrounding villages and countryside and find food and lodging, because we are in a remote place here."*

¹³*He replied, "You give them something to eat."*

They answered, "We have only five loaves of bread and two fish—unless we go and buy food for all this crowd." ¹⁴*(About five thousand men were there.)*

But he said to his disciples, "Have them sit down in groups of about fifty each." ¹⁵*The disciples did so, and everyone sat down.* ¹⁶*Taking the five loaves and the two fish and looking up to heaven, he gave thanks and broke them. Then he gave them to the disciples to distribute to the people.* ¹⁷*They all ate and were satisfied, and the disciples picked up twelve basketfuls of broken pieces that were left over.*

Luke 9:12-17

One time my class went on a field trip to the State Capitol. When we got inside the building, a parent instructed us to give our lunches to the teacher. These were stored in a big crate so later we would easily find them. This seemed like a good idea, but my lunch got lost somewhere in the mix of all the lunches! I was worried about it.

Many kids were willing to give things out of their lunch so I wouldn't go hungry. There were more peanut butter and jam sandwiches than you would know what to do with! This reminded me of Luke 9:12-17. All those people were without lunch too. Jesus provided for them by performing a miracle. Jesus took care of me by providing my lunch, just like He did in the New Testament! Jesus always takes care of our needs.

By: A Kid with Enough Lunch

More from God: Philippians 4:19

Journal Prompt: How has God provided for you?

Butterfly Stomach

Whoever is ashamed of me and my words, the Son of Man will be ashamed of them when he comes in his glory and in the glory of the Father and of the holy angels.

Luke 9:26

Have you ever been ashamed of knowing Jesus? Well, I have. One night, we had friends come over for dinner. While they were over, I had to do some devotions which involved reading a chapter from Matthew.

When I was reading my devotion, one of the girls looked over and saw me reading the Bible. She had a weird look on her face, and I felt like she didn't think it was cool. I just felt like she didn't like that I was reading the Bible.

When they left, I decided to talk to my Mom and Dad about it. They said that I shouldn't be embarrassed about reading God's Word. I should be proud of reading the Bible.

I thought about it and I decided that I was excited to read the Bible, not ashamed or embarrassed. It is truth and everyone needs to hear it. Jesus is important to me, and I want others to know that too.

By: Angelina (United States)

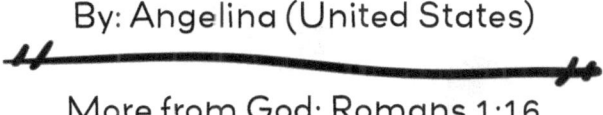

More from God: Romans 1:16

Journal Prompt: Why should you not be ashamed of God's Word?

The Good Samaritans

³⁰In reply Jesus said: "A man was going down from Jerusalem to Jericho, when he was attacked by robbers. They stripped him of his clothes, beat him and went away, leaving him half dead. ³¹A priest happened to be going down the same road, and when he saw the man, he passed by on the other side. ³²So too, a Levite, when he came to the place and saw him, passed by on the other side. ³³But a Samaritan, as he traveled, came where the man was; and when he saw him, he took pity on him.

Luke 10:30-33

The Good Samaritan had pity on someone who didn't have help and was in need. This is a story about when someone was a Good Samaritan to my own family! It was Christmas Eve, and my family was getting ready for bed.

After getting my pajamas on, I looked under the

Christmas tree. There was one gift under the tree. My parents were sad that they didn't have the resources to be able to buy all my siblings gifts. Even so we were thankful we could be together and for one gift under the tree.

The next morning when I woke up, I went to the living room. I yelled, "Mom, get out here!" There were 12 presents under the tree for all of us! I got a baby doll and my very first Bible. I had wanted my own Bible for years since I became a Christian! God really blessed my family that day. Whoever that Good Samaritan was, they showed the love of God to us that day and took pity on our sadness. They reached out and went far beyond what was needed to make us feel special. I will never forget this and now ask that God would help me to look for ways to be a Good Samaritan to others.

By: Amanda (United States)

More from God: Luke 10:34-37

Journal Prompt: Has God ever blessed you with a Good Samaritan in your life? How can you do the same for others?

Don't Be Jealous

²⁵"Meanwhile, the older son was in the field. When he came near the house, he heard music and dancing. ²⁶So he called one of the servants and asked him what was going on. ²⁷'Your brother has come,' he replied, 'and your father has killed the fattened calf because he has him back safe and sound.'

²⁸"The older brother became angry and refused to go in. So his father went out and pleaded with him. ²⁹But he answered his father, 'Look! All these years I've been slaving for you and never disobeyed your orders. Yet you never gave me even a young goat so I could celebrate with my friends.

Luke 15:25-29

This story is about a prodigal son. The prodigal son ran away from his family and got into a lot of trouble. He finally returned home and asked for forgiveness. His dad forgave him and welcomed him back, but his brother was not so happy about it.

He was jealous. Jealousy causes all kinds of problems because we get our minds off God and on ourselves.

I've been jealous a bunch of times too. One time I was jealous of my baby cousin, Victoria. It seemed like she got all the attention. I felt left out and unimportant. My Grandma asked me what was wrong. I told her that everything was okay. I prayed and God helped me not to be jealous. I started helping out with Victoria and spending more time with her. Now I can't wait to see her again. God helped me work through the jealousy and think about helping my grandma and loving Victoria more. God is good—welcoming us back when we do the wrong thing and helps us not to be jealous.

By: Alex (United States)

More from God: James 3:16

Journal Prompt: Why is it important not to be jealous of others?

Stealing is Not Appealing

³ So watch yourselves.

"If your brother or sister sins against you, rebuke them; and if they repent, forgive them. ⁴Even if they sin against you seven times in a day and seven times come back to you saying 'I repent,' you must forgive them."

Luke 17:3-4

Have you ever felt really bad about taking something that wasn't yours? One day back when I was in kindergarten, I was at school lying on my rest mat. I saw something blue. I knew that it was not mine, but I took it anyway. I put it in my pocket and fell asleep. Later that day I felt really bad. I told my mom and put it on the counter.

Unfortunately, school had ended for the summer, and I could not see my teacher to tell her what I had done. About five years later I was able to give it back to her. It made me feel so much better! After giving the toy back, I felt really good inside. I know God forgave me and so did my teacher. He will forgive you too if you repent or say you are sorry to God for wrong things you have done.

Jesus tells us two important things: to repent and forgive others. I'm thankful that Jesus forgives us daily for the wrong things that we do, and in turn we can forgive others too.

By: Baylee (United States)

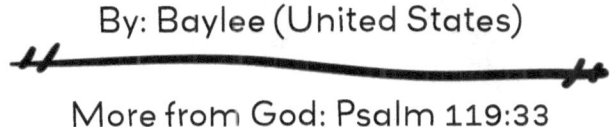

More from God: Psalm 119:33

Journal Prompt: What is God asking you to do in Luke 17:3-4?

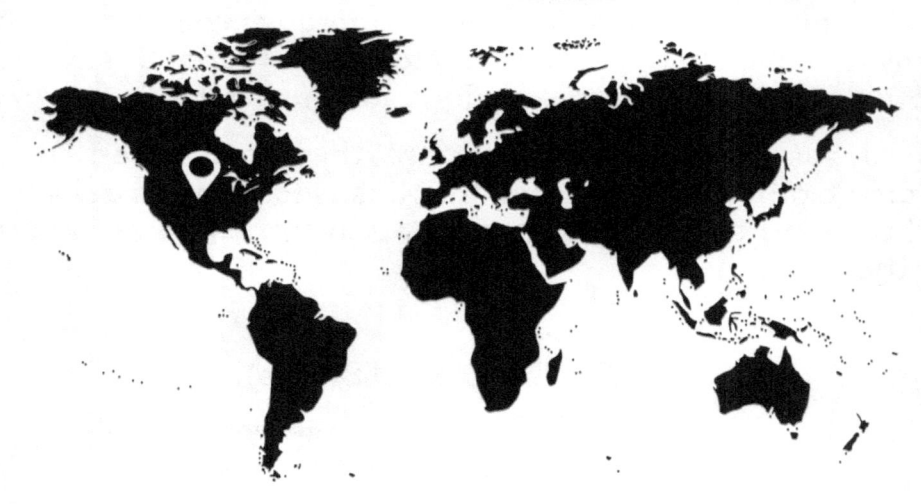

Left Out

A man was there by the name of Zacchaeus; he was a chief tax collector and was wealthy.

Luke 19:2

Have you ever been left out? One day I was walking around the playground. I was having a bad day so then I went to the swings. Someone came up and said, "Hey can you get off the swing?"

I said, "Yes." The day seemed to be getting worse by the minute! I felt lonely. I thought about Zacchaeus sitting up in the tree all by himself feeling alone too.

Then a girl named Baylee came over and asked me if I wanted to play with her! I said, "Yes!" Baylee really cared for me that day! She reached out to me like Jesus reached out to Zacchaeus when he was lonely. She became my friend.

I'm sure Zacchaeus was happy to be included with Jesus that day since as a tax collector he was not very popular. Jesus looks for the lonely and invites them to come and hang out with Him! I'm thankful Jesus saw me in my loneliness too. He is my best friend.

By: Amanda (United States)

More from God: Mark 1:17

Journal Prompt: Journal about a time when you felt left out, and someone reached out to include you. How can you do that for others?

Cheesecake

I am going to send you what my Father has promised; but stay in the city until you have been clothed with power from on high.

Luke 24:49

After Jesus went up to heaven, God promised to give His followers the Holy Spirit. (Ephesians 1:13-14) The Holy Spirit convicts us of our sins, helps us to understand God's Word, and even gives us comfort.

Have you ever felt guilty? One day I was on a special diet in which I could only eat meat and veggies! I saw a cheesecake sitting on the counter. I couldn't resist taking a bite. It was so good I couldn't resist eating more. I ate half! My dad came while I was not there. He yelled, "Who ate my cheesecake?" My family all came downstairs and saw it was half gone. They were staring in disbelief! (I did not realize that I ate half of it). It all happened so fast! I got in very big trouble. I felt guilty.

The Lord brought Luke 24:49 to my mind. God gave us the Holy Spirit which He promised to help us do what is right and give us guidance. Next time I will listen to what God's Spirit prompts me to do. I'm thankful that even when I mess up, God will forgive me and give me the power to do the right thing. He is always there with me no matter what temptation may come along.

By: Caleb (United States)

More from God: Galatians 2:22-23

Journal Prompt: Who can you count on to help you to do the right thing? How do you know?

John

Part 4:
Background to John

John, whom Jesus did love, believed in only the Savior above.

Even though John wrote the book, his name never appears in the Gospel. John was the younger brother of James, (Acts 12:2), and the two were nicknamed, "the sons of Zebedee." (Matthew 10:2-4) John's purpose for writing this Gospel is stated in John 20:30-31, "These are written that you may believe that Jesus is the Christ, the Son of God, and that believing you may have life in His name."

John was a faithful follower of Christ, and even wrote Scripture into his old age as he was outcast on the island of Patmos for sharing the Gospel. Even on this island, man could not stop him from writing God's truth. God loved John and John loved God. The rest is history. As you read these devotions you will see the love of God lived out in lives then and now.

Unbe-reef-able

³Through him all things were made; without him nothing was made that has been made. ⁴In him was life, and that life was the light of all mankind. ⁵The light shines in the darkness, and the darkness has not overcome it.

John 1:3-5

Last week, my cousin and I went on a summer vacation to Mexico with my Mom and Dad. We stayed for a whole week. I was so excited the last day because we were going snorkeling way out in the ocean. When we went, we had to jump off the boat. The thought of cold water scared me, but when I jumped in, it wasn't bad. We swam a little way to a really big reef. I thought it was hard because water kept getting in my mouth and just a little in my eyes, but I had goggles on.

When we got to the second reef, I was looking at the unique fish and as the sunlight shone down it reflected all the beautifully colored coral. It made me think about how creative God is, and all the amazing things He has made. Only the God of the universe could make something this beautiful and perfect! He is the light that shines to help us see and comprehend all the wonderful things He has made for us. That's when I remembered John 1:3-5. When I told my Mom, Dad, and cousin they said, "Wow I really never thought about that." God truly is amazing.

By: Angelina (United States)

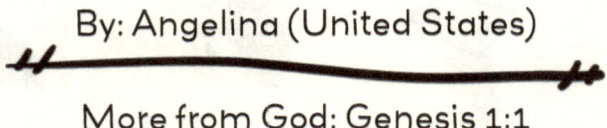

More from God: Genesis 1:1

Journal Prompt: Look around you today. Notice the things God has made. Write out a prayer to thank God for your life and the beautiful creation He gave us.

My Testimony

¹In the beginning was the Word, and the Word was with God, and the Word was God. ²He was with God in the beginning. ³Through him all things were made; without him nothing was made that has been made. ⁴In him was life, and that life was the light of all mankind. ⁵The light shines in the darkness, and the darkness has not overcome it.

John 1:1-5

My name is Beatriz, and I had a problem. I didn't understand how God created the world and who created him and how God is three in one. (God the Father, God the Son and God the Holy Spirit). So, I decided to read the Bible.

I found out in John 3:16 that God loved the world and gave His Son so we could have eternal life. I realized Jesus died on the cross for me and that God is my Savior and is saving me from my sins. I believe the Bible isn't just made-up stories. But it was written by God, not someone else communicating to us.

Some people might think that God is a joke, but I know God is real. The Gospel is for all people no matter who you are. I choose to believe the truth in the Bible, pray and worship Him and only Him.

By: Beatriz (Dominican Republic)

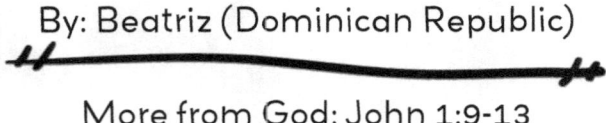

More from God: John 1:9-13

Journal Prompt: What truth have you learned from the Bible?

I Want To Be Like That

Yet to all who did receive him, to those who believed in his name, he gave the right to become children of God

John 1:12

Have you ever felt like somebody is better than you at something? Sometimes I feel this way. Sometimes I feel left out when someone has better clothes, is better at singing, or better at video games. I compare myself and start to feel bad. I start thinking "I want to be like that."

It even happened at camp. There was a drawing contest and the winner got two packs of Starbursts. I thought it would be fun just to draw a picture. So, my friends and I signed up. We got paper, crayons, markers, and colored pencils.

While I was coloring, I looked over my shoulder and noticed both of my friends were coloring the most awesome pictures! I looked at my picture of a simple flower and thought it was nothing special. I felt like everybody was better than me. I was comparing myself to others.

I went back to my cabin and read some of my Bible. When I read about being a child of God, it made me feel special. Because I have received Christ as my Savior, I am God's child. This makes me very important because He created me for a purpose. The God of the universe calls me His child! God, who created everything, doesn't make mistakes. I can be thankful for the way He made me and the abilities He has given to me. This helps me to not compare myself with others and to be thankful for all the blessings Jesus gives to me! I can also be happy for the talents God gave others.

By: Kamille (United States)

More from God: Ephesians 1:3-8

Journal Prompt: Write about a time you had an "I Want to Be Like That" Story.

I'm Angry

¹³When it was almost time for the Jewish Passover, Jesus went up to Jerusalem. ¹⁴In the temple courts he found people selling cattle, sheep and doves, and others sitting at tables exchanging money. ¹⁵So he made a whip out of cords, and drove all from the temple courts, both sheep and cattle; he scattered the coins of the money changers and overturned their tables. ¹⁶To those who sold doves he said, "Get these out of here! Stop turning my Father's house into a market!" ¹⁷His disciples remembered that it is written: "Zeal for your house will consume me."

John 2:13-17

Have you ever been angry? It's ok to be angry sometimes. Jesus was angry because of sin that was happening. It is important to choose what in life is worth getting angry about and make wise choices about how we express our anger.

My mom says, "Life is too short to get angry," and she is right! If we spend our lives getting angry about all of the little things, we will miss out on what God has in store for us. Those things are worth standing up for!

Jesus got angry, but for good reason. The people were using the temple for buying and selling instead of worshiping God. Jesus came in and wrecked everything and gave the people a lecture. Jesus taught by example. He loved the people enough to show them how important it was to worship God first.

We can get angry about some things and even try to fix them, but we have to handle our anger in the same way Jesus did. We have to still love the people and stay in control. I sometimes get mad at my brother and he gets mad at me and then we get out of control and treat each other badly. This anger is not pleasing to God.

By: Benjamin (United States)

More from God: Luke 15:28

Journal Prompt: Whenever you get angry, remember to ask God for help to handle your anger in a way that is pleasing to Him. Write a prayer to God about this.

Believe It or Not

For God so loved the world that he gave his one and only Son, that whoever believes in him shall not perish but have eternal life.

John 3:16

Have you ever been thankful that God gave His one and only son? Well, I have. I am going to tell you my testimony. After I realized I needed God's forgiveness, I started to be very thankful for Jesus.

It all started when I was in my room lying on my bed, thinking about what my life would be like if I committed it to Jesus. I kind of had a bad attitude at first. I thought everything about God, Jesus, and the Holy Spirit was all fake! I didn't want to be a person who believes in false things.

But then my mom read the story in the Bible about when Jesus was tempted by Satan. (I almost never read the Bible with my mom, but this time she sat down with me to read.) Then my mom left my room. After that, I thought about all the bad things (sins) that I had done. I needed help and wanted forgiveness for those sins. At that point, I knew God was real. I believed Jesus died for my sins and that He was God's one and only Son, and I was thankful that Jesus came to earth. He took on my sins and even gave His life for me even though I did not deserve it. That is an amazing God. I committed my life to Jesus that day. I felt a great peace fill my heart after knowing the truth.

By: Anonymous (United States)

More from God: Romans 3:23

Journal Prompt: Where do you find truth?

Jesus Died For Me

For God so loved the world that he gave his one and only Son, that whoever believes in him shall not perish but have eternal life.

John 3:16

Every time I feel sad, I remember that God gave His only son because He loves me so much. It says in John 3:16 that if we believe in His Son, we are given eternal life.

I also think about this when I want to do something that is not right, because Jesus died for my salvation I should follow his commandments so that his death would have a purpose in my life and glorify Him.

He loved me enough to sacrifice (act of offering) himself for my sins and now I can live knowing and following Him. What other god would give up himself to do this for us?

By: Ana Lucia (Dominican Republic)

More from God: Psalm 86:12-13

Journal Prompt: What would you do to honor Jesus' sacrifice? Think about it and journal what you are thinking.

VBS Changed My Life

For God did not send his Son into the world to condemn the world, but to save the world through him.

John 3:17

Once, I was at Maxwell Airforce Base in Alabama. It was my first day at a Vacation Bible School. This is like a day camp they have at church where kids do activities and learn about Jesus. I went to the meeting room and found my group, and we played a whole bunch of fun games, sang songs, and prayed. We did things like this all week. My favorite part was when we prayed and sang.

Back then, I didn't know Jesus Christ, so I thought praying and singing were just talking and playing games, but the last day changed my life. On the last day I was having a lot of fun, and everyone went to a meeting room. I followed, and when I got there, they were about to start an awards ceremony.

I sat with my group. Then all of a sudden, they called

my name and I was startled! I went on stage and they gave a Bible. They encouraged me by saying they saw me singing and praying.

Right then and there I realized who I was singing and praying for! I prayed and really talked to Jesus and wanted to follow Him. He is what my whole life and soul are about now! I pray, sing, walk and talk with Jesus every single day! God saved me that day and my life will never be the same.

By: Maddie (United States)

More from God: Galatians 2:20

Journal Prompt: Is your life all about Jesus Christ? If so, how does that affect your day?

Becoming God's Child

Whoever believes in him is not condemned, but whoever does not believe stands condemned already because they have not believed in the name of God's one and only Son.

John 3:18

Have you ever had a time when you felt lonely inside? I did at a very young age. I went to my first day of kindergarten. I stepped into the room; I had no friends. It was very scary and lonely. It seemed like all I wanted to do was just cry, but I held it together.

I went to Chapel the next day. They told me about Jesus. I learned that if I believed in God's one and only Son, I would be saved. I decided to pray and I became Christian!

Now I will never be lonely again, even if no one is with me, because Jesus is with me every day. He and I hang out together and talk. He is my best friend.

Anyone can be a Christian and have a best friend in Jesus if you pray to God and believe in the name of Jesus, God's one and only Son. Even in kindergarten I realized this, and I'm so glad I did!

By: Bella (United States)

More from God: John 3:17

Journal Prompt: Do you believe in Jesus as your Savior? If so, write a note to Jesus thanking Him for being your best friend.

The Soccer Story

Jesus gave them this answer: "Very truly I tell you, the Son can do nothing by himself; he can do only what he sees his Father doing, because whatever the Father does the Son also does.

John 5:19

Have you ever thought you could make it without God? Once I thought I could do a soccer game without God's help or praying before it.

It was a prideful thing. Then I realized I needed God's help for everything I do. Whether getting slide-tackled, losing, scoring, or winning, it is all for God's glory.

He gives me strength and helps me to do my best so God can be praised no matter the outcome. With God, I can have a good attitude and show His ove by encouraging others even when the game is not going the way I wanted.

When you think you can do things on your own, you will find fear and disappointment. Jesus even knew He could do nothing without the Father. Now I pray to God before everything I do and praise Him for how He helps me to do it with all my heart as for Him. (Proverbs 3:5-6)

By: Tim (United States)

More about God: Acts 17:28

Journal Prompt: What is it that you are trying to do on your own without God? Write a prayer asking Him for strength so others see God in what you do.

I Was Awestruck

Very truly I tell you, whoever hears my word and believes him who sent me has eternal life and will not be judged but has crossed over from death to life.

John 5:24

Before I knew Christ, I was the mean popular girl at school, but refused to admit it. My faith was always an afterthought in my life. I thought that because I grew up in a Christian home I was saved. Then everything I had held onto in life fell apart. I moved churches and schools at the same time, which to a kid is like the end of the world. No one wants to be the new kid. My new school was full of Christians who always talked about God and what was right and wrong, but I thought I knew more about God than them. I was soon proved wrong, and over the next year I was frustrated that I didn't know as much about the Bible as my friends. I acted like God didn't exist but blamed Him when things went badly.

During this time, I thought that whenever I sinned, God rejected me. In Sunday school at our new church, I thought I would hear the same Bible stories that I was used to, but the teacher did a lesson on Romans 3:23, "For all have sinned and fallen short of the glory God." She said that we all have sinned against God and there is nothing we can do to stop the punishment of death. I was awestruck. That was the point in my life when I finally understood the truth. I needed Jesus who died on the cross for the punishment of my sins.

From then on, I started to take notes and pay attention to the pastor's sermon. I started to see myself growing more spiritually mature. Over the past year I have put my trust in Jesus who died and rose again so that I may spend eternity with him. I know that if I were to die today, I would be in Heaven with Him.

By Brynnley (United States)

More from God: Luke 23:44-48

Journal Prompt: What is so amazing about Jesus paying the punishment for our sins?

Don't Be Afraid

But he said to them, "It is I; don't be afraid."

John 6:20

Camp Elim is a beautiful summer camp in the mountains of Colorado. My dad was leading and working there for the week, and even though I was not old enough to be a camper, I got to go along to help.

We just got done with singing in the chapel, and he left to go to the trailer to get a Diet Coke. It had been an hour, and my dad wasn't back yet, and I was about to get scared. I went to the trailer. He wasn't there! I prayed to God to help me not to be afraid.

Next, I went to the office and asked Aunt Terrie if she had seen my dad. She said, "No." I went around the playground and then I looked in the pool area. He wasn't there either! Then I looked around the campgrounds and I couldn't find him, so I went to the trailer and cleaned a little of it, trying not to worry, but instead thinking of Jesus.

I then walked back to the chapel and my dad was there! It was such a good feeling to be with him and not have that fear inside. My dad told me he was sorry that we didn't get to go watch the campers' games.

"It's ok," I said. So we did sound testing for the chapel and when it was time to sing, we sang worship songs. Jesus helped me to not be afraid when I kept thinking about him. Even when we are not right near our earthly father, we can always be with our heavenly Father and He will take away any fear.

By: Amanda (United States)

More from God: Zechariah 13:9

Journal Prompt: When was a time you felt alone or afraid?

Stressed or Blessed?

The next day the crowd that had stayed on the opposite shore of the lake realized that only one boat had been there, and that Jesus had not entered it with his disciples, but that they had gone away alone.

John 6:22

One day I was busy, and I had a lot of work to do at my house. I kept worrying about what to do next, and I wasn't focused on what I was supposed to do, so I got really stressed. Then I remembered that my dad always told me to spend quiet time with God to read His Word and pray. I was really tired and wanted to watch TV instead. When I looked around, nobody was watching so I disobeyed my dad and watched TV.

When my dad asked me if I had done my devotion, I told him that I had not done it. My dad then asked me to spend the day in my room without electronics so I would think about what was most important.'

Later I started spending quiet time with God, and I was not mad anymore. I drew closer to God with each story from the Bible I read. I also did my chores and wasn't angered or stressed in the work I did.

Jesus modeled getting away to spend quiet time talking to God. Some people try to ignore spending time alone with God like I did. Jesus wants us to take time to read His Word and hang out with Him. I learned it is important to take time to be with God.

By: Melanie (United States)

More from God: 2 Timothy 3:16-17

Journal Prompt: How much time do you spend hanging out with God and reading God's Word? How can you rearrange your day to do more of this?

Happy as a King

Then Jesus declared, "I am the bread of life. Whoever comes to me will never go hungry, and whoever believes in me will never be thirsty."

John 6:35

I was an orphan girl because my mother died and there was no one to take care of me. I didn't know how I would eat or live. I was living such a troubled life. Then Pastor Richard came one day and took me to an orphanage. This is a place where they feed and help children without parents. Now I am happy as a king! I have food to eat and people praying for me every day.

The first day at the orphanage, I went to church and heard about how much God loved me. The pastor prayed with me to receive Christ as my Savior. Jesus now takes care of all my needs, and I do not need to worry anymore. He is my everything. God showed me personally how He is my bread of life just like John 6:35 says.

By: Inspired by Anna (Kenya)

More from God: John 14:6

Journal Prompt: What does John 6:35 mean to you? Journal about it.

Forgiveness

In John 8:5-12, Jesus forgives a woman caught in adultery. Jesus went to the temple to preach. The teachers of the law brought a woman out who was caught in adultery. They forced the woman to stand in front of the people.

> [5]In the Law Moses commanded us to stone such women. Now what do you say?" [6]They were using this question as a trap, in order to have a basis for accusing him.
>
> But Jesus bent down and started to write on the ground with his finger. [7]When they kept on questioning him, he straightened up and said to them, "Let any one of you who is without sin be the first to throw a stone at her." [8]Again he stooped down and wrote on the ground.
>
> [9]At this, those who heard began to go away one at a time, the older ones first, until only Jesus was left, with the woman still standing there. [10]Jesus straightened up and asked

her, *"Woman, where are they? Has no one condemned you?"*

[11]*"No one, sir,"* she said.

"Then neither do I condemn you," Jesus declared. *"Go now and leave your life of sin."*

Jesus forgives us just as He forgave the woman in that story. I have two sisters that I fight with a lot. We get into arguments and yell at each other. I need God to forgive me all the time.

If you need God to forgive you, all you have to do is ask and He will gladly forgive you always. Everyone needs God's forgiveness sometimes because everyone sins. Jesus forgives and teaches us not to judge because if we look closely, we probably do the same thing.

By: Dylan (United States)

More from God: Luke 6:37

Journal Prompt: Think about a time when you needed forgiveness. What did you do?

Sparkle on the Inside

Jesus answered, "Even if I testify on my own behalf, my testimony is valid, for I know where I came from and where I am going. But you have no idea where I come from or where I am going."

John 8:14

Jesus knew who He was and where He came from. He was the Son of God and came to earth to fulfill God's plan. Even though the Scribes and Pharisees (religious leaders) in Jesus' day perceived Him like He was nothing special-Jesus spoke with certainty of who He was.

There is a really pretty rock called a geode. It's very beautiful on the inside, but the outside is nothing special. When some people look at it, they think it's not worth anything. They may just walk by, not notice, and leave it, or even kick it out of the way or discard it, not believing it is anything special.

Maybe you have seen one. There are also people who

pick it up, take it home and break it open. When they see the inside, they realize how spectacular and beautiful it is!

It's kind of like people. We may judge others by their looks or put down others when we don't really know them from outside appearances. Maybe we feel like we are not pretty or handsome enough.

When Jesus is in your life, you know who you are in Christ no matter what people say. Maybe you don't think people perceive who you really are or think you are beautiful on the outside. Whenever you don't feel beautiful, think about the sparkle on the inside. That is what really counts. When others get to know you, they will see your testimony of where you came from and where you are going. In other words, they will see how God has made you and what He has asked you to do. This is the true beauty of Jesus sparkling through and others will be amazed at the inner beauty that only comes from Jesus within. I'm glad Jesus testified on His own behalf and rose in glory. We can sparkle knowing Him and that glory too!

Go ahead, testify on God's behalf and sparkle from the inside. Others will see His glory coming through.

By: Elle (United States)

More from God: Isaiah 45:24

Journal Prompt: Where does your value come from? Do you know who you are in Christ? Write about it.

Hardship Happens

¹As he went along, he saw a man blind from birth. ²His disciples asked him, "Rabbi, who sinned, this man or his parents, that he was born blind?"

³"Neither this man nor his parents sinned," said Jesus, "but this happened so that the works of God might be displayed in him.

John 9:1-3

"All things work together for good to those who love the Lord." (Romans 8:28) Even though things can be hard, we can trust God is sovereign and sees the whole picture.

One Sunday, my friend and I were playing in my neighborhood. My dad said to come home at a certain time so we wouldn't be late for the play rehearsal at my church. I was having so much fun, I lost track of time, so my dad came in the car to tell me we needed to go. In the rush, I forgot to put my helmet on, so I ran with my bike and right in front of me was a rock. I tripped on it and the handlebar pushed my eye back. I screamed! My dad turned around thinking it was just a scrape. When he saw that my face was all bloody, he helped me in the car quickly and we went back to my house. When we cleaned off   my face, we could see something was wrong so we went to church to tell someone I wouldn't make it to rehearsals. Then we went over to urgent care. We waited in a room for what seemed like a long time. Then they said it was so bad that they couldn't do anything, and I needed to go to the hospital. It was across the street, so my dad rushed me there. They took X-rays and they saw my skull was broken in two different spots behind my eye and by my nose. The doctor said it was amazing that I would not have to have surgery, but they would check it every day for a week. God was faithful to take care of me and show Himself mighty in my life to others.

The doctors saw the works of God being displayed through my injury. Sometimes bad things happen to us, just like the blind man Jesus talked about in John chapter nine. God can use these things to show others His great and mighty works. Read the rest of the story to see what happened to the blind man in John 9:5-12.

By: Faith (United States)

More from God: Psalm 37:3

Journal Prompt: How has God displayed His mighty works through hardship in your life?

Hello, Are You Listening?

My sheep listen to my voice; I know them, and they follow me.

John 10:27

Do you ever wonder if God hears you and pays attention to you?

Well, I've wondered about that very thing. I've prayed to God many times before, but after a while I wondered if He was really listening. I found out the answer to that is, absolutely! Every single thought you think and every word you say, God hears. That really makes you think, doesn't it? To imagine that the God of the universe hears and knows us better than we know ourselves is a little over whelming.

Sometimes after thinking about this, we realize that we probably haven't been pleasing God and listening to Him. No worries - just apologize to God and follow what He tells you to do. Ask God to forgive you for the bad things you've done and spend time getting to know Him better by reading your Bible and praying. When you get to know

Him better, you understand how much He does hear you and cares about everything concerning you. He wants so much to have a friendship with us and for us to know His voice. He does pay attention to us; we just need to slow down and listen to Him.

By: Jennifer (United States)

More from God: Psalm 85:8

Journal Prompt: How do you spend time just listening to God?

Don't Be Afraid!

My Father, who has given them to me, is greater than all; no one can snatch them out of my Father's hand.

John 10:29

Sometimes we all feel afraid. I have felt fear many times, and I'm sure you have too. One time, my family wanted to look at a couple of different houses to buy. After we looked at the houses, my parents kept talking privately in their room.

I was really scared because I didn't want to move away from my friends. Fear gripped me. I tried to look on the bright side, but there was no bright side in my mind.

Then I heard a voice in my head repeating over and over saying, "Don't be afraid because I am with you." John 10:29 tells us that no matter where we go, no one or no circumstance can take you away from God.

Even if I moved, God would not move from me! He would give me strength and courage wherever I go. In His hands, I can have peace inside.

By: Melanie (United States)

More from God: Isaiah 41:10

Journal Prompt: Why should I talk to God when I am afraid?

My Own Testimony

Very truly I tell you, whoever accepts anyone I send accepts me; and whoever accepts me accepts the one who sent me.

John 13:20

When you read through the book of John, it seems much of it is about people sharing their testimony, or what happened when they received Jesus into their life. Jesus did many great things for the people in the New Testament. The most important thing was when they realized that Jesus died on the cross to pay the penalty for their sin. He also did not stay dead but rose again! Those people went out and told others about it. It made me think about the great thing Jesus has done for me and my own testimony.

When I was little, I always wondered about many things, such as why we had to do Communion and learn about Jesus Christ, eat bread and drink grape juice. My first time reading the Bible, I thought that it was just a book with stories about Jesus and all kinds of characters. Then at my Church, the teacher kept on saying these things I didn't understand; such things like how Noah listened to a guy named God. I thought, was this really important? Then I heard the story about Jesus' death, and the thought went through my mind that He did this all just for me! A few months later, I received Jesus into my life. This happened at a place called Camp Elim in Colorado. God blessed me at that camp like nobody's business.

Just like the people in the book of John, I too have a testimony to share with others about how I received the truth of who Jesus was, sent by God to save the world. Now I am excited to share that with others!

By: Amanda (United States)

More from God: John 14:6

Journal Prompt: What is your testimony?

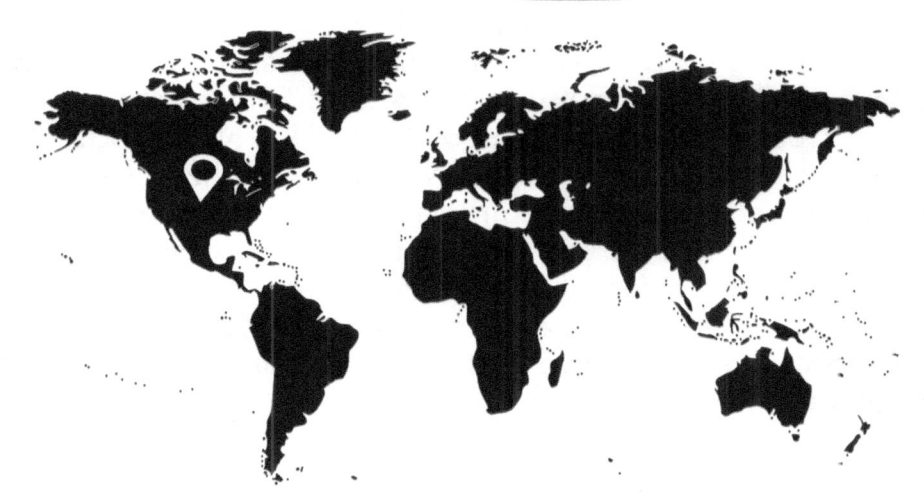

Swim Classic

Do not let your hearts be troubled. You believe in God; believe also in me.

John 14:1

Have you ever been uncomfortable or troubled when people are different than you?

A guy named Jimmy Flowers climbed a mountain one day and unfortunately fell off in a fatal accident. Before Jimmy's time came, he did some amazing things. He got married, raised two kids, and trained people for the Paralympics. This is when people who are disabled, compete in special competitions. Jimmy trained people for the swimming category. And in honor of him, they hold a Paralympics Swim Meet each year.

The first year I went to this event, I was kind of freaked out how some people looked. The next time, however, was different. When my dad and I first got there, I was still uncomfortable, but something I saw changed my mind. There was this 11-year-old girl. She had no legs, was missing an arm, and even the arm she did have was crippled. Do you know what she did? She swam all the way across the swimming pool. I could barely do that, and I have all my limbs! At that moment, I realized that just because people have certain disadvantages in life, doesn't mean they can't do the normal stuff we do. God uses all kinds of people for whatever He chooses. God doesn't make mistakes. I believe God has a plan for each person He created and can give them grace to meet whatever He asks them to do.

By: Luke (United States)

More from God: 2 Corinthians 13:14

Journal Prompt: Describe a time when your heart was troubled but you still believed in God's plan.

Everything New

*My Father's house has many rooms; if that were not so,
would I have told you that I am going there to prepare a place
for you?*

John 14:2

Have you ever truly thought about what heaven would be like? I've thought a lot about it and, from reading John 14:2, heaven should be a great place. There are many opinions about what heaven will be like. I have heard that heaven is where we get a mansion and can fly. Some people wonder if you know what is going on down on earth while in heaven. People think a lot of different things about what heaven will be like, but that is not what's most important. What we really will care about is that when we go to heaven Jesus will be there, and we get to worship Him all day! Seeing His awesomeness will naturally bring paise!

Funny, some people think they can just hope for the best whether they will go to heaven or not, but I know the only way to get to heaven is to believe in Jesus. (John 3:16) All that being said, I seriously look forward to heaven being the best time of my life. After all, God has prepared it and He is a pretty creative, magnificent God! How awesome it is for Him to do that for us! Hopefully I will see you there too!

By: Owen (United States)

More from God: Revelation 21

Journal Prompt: What do you think heaven will be like?

God Is Your Helper

But the Advocate, the Holy Spirit, whom the Father will send in my name, will teach you all things and will remind you of everything I have said to you.

John 14:26

God is good to give us an awesome helper to prompt us to remember His truth and promises.

Has something in your life ever gone wrong? Once, my dad called a family meeting. My dad said, "I know we have just been to our relative's house, and everything was good. Well, I have some sad news. Our relatives are getting a divorce."

I thought to myself, how could this happen? I didn't know what to do. Then I remembered that God sent a helper, the Holy Spirit, to be there for me when things are out of my control. God knows what to do even when I do not. He cares about every little problem and will see me through even when it is hard to understand. He is still working in this situation, and I know He will be there for support and strength.

Whenever you feel like things are hard and God is not with you, remember to ask the Holy Spirit for help. God will keep His promise to give you what you need and be your helper in tough times.

By: Hope (United States)

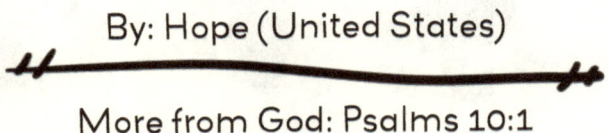

More from God: Psalms 10:1

Journal Prompt: Name a time when you needed to trust God through something difficult happening to you or someone around you.

I'm Worried

Peace I leave with you; my peace I give you. I do not give to you as the world gives. Do not let your hearts be troubled and do not be afraid.

John 14:27

Have you ever been worried? It is a normal thing that everyone has felt at times. But you shouldn't be worried because God is always with you.

One night I was at my neighbor's house sleeping over because my baby sister was being born. I was worried. I didn't know what was going on. My neighbor was sound asleep, and I felt very alone. I tried not to think about it and looked at the pictures in a book until I fell asleep.

My dad came during the night and carried me back home while I was sleeping. The next morning, I woke up in my bed. I got up to see if my sister was there. I asked my dad and he said she was still in the hospital and would be home in a few days.

I continued to worry about it. Then I read John 14:27.

I realized God would take care of me and my new sister. He cared about everything about us! I felt like God was helping me not to worry. My sister did come home, and I thank God for the way He always takes care of us.

By: Bella (United States)

More from God: Psalm 16:8

Journal Prompt: What does John 14:27 mean to you?

Everybody is a Winner

As the Father has loved me, so have I loved you. Now remain in my love.

John 15:9

Have you ever felt like you are not loved?

One day I was at a track meet with a couple of guys, and we were racing. When the whistle blew, I know this sounds crazy, but I got messed up and ran the wrong way! So, I turned around and started running the right way. But by that time, the other contestants were about halfway to the finish line! I started running as hard as I could. Even though I did not win, and felt that others were laughing at me, I still got a ribbon for participation.

God helped me see something even though I lost. This race reminded me of how much God loves me even though I go the wrong direction. He does not laugh at me or throw me out of the race. When we remain in His love, like I remained in the race, He shows us His love and acceptance even when we go the wrong direction or mess up! He loves us no matter what! I'm glad about that because we all have those times when we need to turn around and go the right way. God helped me to see His love for me and He will help you too!

By: Joel (United States)

More from God: Hebrews 13:5

Journal Prompt: Think about a time when you felt God's prompting and love when you were headed the wrong direction.

Failing Friendship

My command is this: Love each other as I have loved you.

John 15:12

John 15:12 is a hard thing to do, especially in friendships.

Friendships can be tricky. Back in first grade, I made a really good friend. We had so much fun! In second grade, though, it was starting to turn into a disaster. I felt like another girl started taking away my best friend! At recess, she would grab my friend's hand and run away with her, leaving me behind. It made me sad that my best friend would go along with this and leave me out. I was really lonely.

Then I started playing with some other girls I had never played with before. Playing with them was surprisingly fun too! I realized it is important to love others as Jesus loves me. That means that I can include everyone, as God loves everyone. God allowed this situation to happen, so I'd learn how to share my friend with others, and make new friends! I'm still friends with all of them- old and new- today. God does miracles beyond me. Life is not always about me, but it is about loving others just as God loves me.

By: Sarah (United States)

More from God: 1 John 4:7

Journal Prompt: Have you ever had a failing friendship? How can you love others through it?

Give it Up

Greater love has no one than this: to lay down one's life for one's friends.

John 15:13

Have you ever had to try to train yourself to stop doing the wrong thing? I am the oldest in my family. I have two younger sisters and I love them very much! In fact, we are usually best friends, but sometimes we fight. This is due to wanting our own way. We can argue about the tiniest things. Sometimes we yell and shout at each other and I lose my temper! My sisters and I at times are not laying down our lives for each other. That takes a lot of work! God tells us to lay down our lives for our friends. This means to think about others more than ourselves.

Philippians 2:14 says to "Do everything without complaining and arguing." We argue and complain too much. We not only argue with each other, but we also complain about dinner often. "Not this again!" we groan.

But sometimes these Scriptures pop into my head. If I am in the middle of a fight, I try to think about the other person, give up what I want and make peace. If I don't like dinner, I try not to complain. My whole family is asking God to help us apply these things to our life. Loving others involves laying down our own will and putting ourselves in their place. I think about what my sister is feeling, or how hard my mom worked preparing dinner. This helps me not to argue and complain.

Family times may be difficult, but God's Word gives us guidance to help us.

By: Dylan (United States)

More from God: Romans 12:18

Journal Prompt: What can you do to lay down your life for family members or others today?

Hot Stuff

But when he, the Spirit of truth, comes, he will guide you into all the truth. He will not speak on his own; he will speak only what he hears, and he will tell you what is yet to come.

John 16:13

Once when I was very young, I didn't know what fire was. I guess all kids need to find out, right? I was supposed to be taking a nap, but snuck away from my bed, looking for mischief. There was a beautiful candle burning on the table that caught my eye. Not being able to reach it, I ran to the bathroom and got my stool to stand on. Then I got so curious that I bent over the candle. My hair fell in the flame! I started to scream because the fire had climbed so high that it touched my cheek! My mom ran in and dipped my head in the sink. God protected me from something very bad. The doctor told my mom I was going to be fine.

God gives us the Holy Spirit as a guide, so we know the truth about things. If we listen to His voice, He steers us away from things that can harm us spiritually. Like with me, sometimes curiosity gets the best of us, and we fall into sin. God gently guides us back through His Holy Spirit and teaches us to follow the truth, just as He taught me to stay away from fire that can hurt me. He teaches us to stay away from things that can harm us and hurt our relationship with Him.

By: Maddie (United States)

More from God: 2 Peter 2:9

Journal Prompt: How has the Holy Spirit guided and protected you from harm?

I Want My Dad

I have told you these things, so that in me you may have peace. In this world you will have trouble. But take heart! I have overcome the world.

John 16:33

When I was younger, my daddy was deployed to another country. He was in the US Navy, and it was so hard to have him gone. He was gone for about a year and two months. I felt sad and broken.

But God was there with me the whole time and He was watching over my daddy. Even though it was hard, it made me stronger and helped me to realize that God had a plan.

God gave me and my family peace when we were apart from my dad. God brought my dad home safely and I am very thankful.

Even when my dad on earth was away, my father (God) in heaven was always there with me. If you trust God, He will always help you.

By: Elle (United States)

More from God: Proverbs 3:5-6

Journal Prompt: How does trusting in God's truth change you?

Twin Day

Now this is eternal life: that they know you, the only true God, and Jesus Christ, whom you have sent.

John 17:3

Do you know God and see His works in the everyday things? God showed me this on a special day called Twin Day at our school.

We have a week at school to build school spirit called, "Spirit Week". During this fun week are special days and one of them is Twin Day, which is filled with students dressed as twins, mirroring someone else. It's like seeing double the whole day!

This day started with a surprising thing only God could orchestrate. As all the kids came walking through the front gate someone noticed something spectacular. It was a double rainbow! The colors were so vivid.

The beautiful twin rainbows stretched from one side of the campus to the other. What happened next was really cool. The students just started jumping and yelling, "Thank you God for giving us twin rainbows on Twin Day!"

God showed us His awesome creation and started our day pointing us to thinking about Him and His promises! Knowing God is truly amazing because you see how the God of the universe knows and cares about us personally in the everyday things.

Inspired by students at Santiago Christian School (Dominican Republic)

More about God: Psalm 121:5-8

Journal Prompt: Do you know God? If so, what ways do you recognize his presence and care for you?

For more information about the school go to:

https://www.scs.edu.do/

Breakfast With Jesus

¹⁵When they had finished eating, Jesus said to Simon Peter, "Simon son of John, do you love me more than these?"

"Yes, Lord," he said, "you know that I love you." Jesus said, "Feed my lambs."

¹⁶Again Jesus said, "Simon son of John, do you love me?" He answered, "Yes, Lord, you know that I love you." Jesus said, "Take care of my sheep."

¹⁷The third time he said to him, "Simon son of John, do you love me?"

Peter was hurt because Jesus asked him the third time, "Do you love me?" He said, "Lord, you know all things; you know that I love you."

Jesus said, "Feed my sheep. ¹⁸Very truly I tell you, when you were younger you dressed yourself and went where you wanted; but when you are old you will stretch out your hands, and someone *else will dress you and lead you where you do not want to go."* [19] *Jesus said this to indicate the kind of death by which Peter would glorify God. Then he said to him, "Follow me!"*

John 21:15-19

After Jesus had risen from the dead, He came to the disciples who were fishing. He helped them catch fish and then invited them to have breakfast with him on the shore. As they were having breakfast, he kept telling Peter over and over, "If you love me, you need to feed my sheep."

I think Jesus meant in this passage that we are to go and help others know the Word of God better. I also think feeding God's sheep means nurturing and helping those who are helpless, like sheep are. God gave me the opportunity to do this when I was younger. I went to my weekly Awana meeting at church, but this one evening people came who were missionaries in Rwanda. They told us of other missionaries whose houses had been burned and all their possessions were gone. They needed help. God prompted me to go home and tell my parents that I wanted to give money (which I had saved for skates) to give to these people.

It was a way I could take care of God's sheep. Even though I was young, God showed me what to do to encourage and help others.

Inspired by Joshua (United States)

More from God: 1 Corinthians 13:2-3

Journal Prompt: What can you do to show God that you love Him?

So That You May Believe

But these are written that you may believe that Jesus is the Messiah, the Son of God, and that by believing you may have life in his name.

John 20:31

I found out in the spring that we were expecting a new baby sister, and I was so excited about it. Then we found out that she had trisomy 13, and we felt very sad. I cried a lot because I knew she would die either before or after she was born. Finally, my mom went to the hospital and she had my baby sister, Christiana Faith. We spent a precious 92 minutes with her until she went to Heaven. She was SO cute! We all got to meet her and hold her at the hospital.

Even though we are sad, we know Christ still loves us. He has written truth for us to know Him in His Word, the Bible. Because Jesus died and rose from the dead, we know we can have eternal life with Him, and that we will see Christiana again.

We also have had the opportunity to share the hope of Christ with other families who have to say goodbye to their babies. We have hope because we believe in Jesus and His love for us all.

By: Evie (United States)

More from God: John 3:16

For more information about our mission, you can visit www.christianafaithfoundation.org

Journal

Epilogue

Walking through the dusty, hot roads of an abandoned neighborhood, I was wondering why God had brought me to this place. Being in a foreign country it was difficult to relate to the language barrier, and I was feeling inadequate as a short-term missionary. Teaching in a classroom with American children was much more in my comfort zone than this. Out of the corner of my eye I saw a small girl. She was standing by a makeshift building that may have seen better days. Noticing her hands and feet were disabled due to a deformity, she looked down continually. God drew me over to her and I wanted our eyes to meet. Through an interpreter we communicated. Wanting our relationship to continue with Smelina, I invited her to a church service in the area we were holding that evening. It seemed the society saw her as an outcast, but God saw her as His child.

That evening the mission team provided a beautiful church service filled with joyful singing and worship to God. My heart broke though as I did not see my new little friend, Smelina. I thought for sure she would come. People were stacking chairs after the service and out of the corner of my eye she appeared. My heart skipped with joy! Immediately, I walked through the crowded room. It was such a blessing to be with her. Later, I escorted her to the leader of the children's program at the church. We were blessed to sign up to be her sponsors so she could go to school, have a meal daily, and receive medical attention.

The whole week while serving at the community center we hung out with Smelina. During that time, Smelina was not keen on smiling and rarely met eyes with anyone. Her hands were always hidden when pictures were taken. In my way of thinking, I thought I knew how to fix things that were difficult for her, such as buying her things I thought she needed. But God prompted me just to make sure she had access to school and a good meal every day. At the end of the week, I gave her a Bible and wrote inside the cover; To Smelina. God loves you so much and so do I. Through an interpreter Smelina prayed a prayer to ask Christ to be her Savior as she wanted to follow Him. That next year, she wrote letters and told me how hard she was working in school.

The next summer, my friend, Diane, went to visit the area where Smelina lived with a group doing service for the church. I sent a gift with Diane to give to Smelina. The day my friend gave the gift was very busy. People were scurrying around in a hot crowded room. Smelina was sitting in a chair and Diane handed her the gift. I had written on the outside of the package in Spanish: To Smelina. God loves you and I love you. I am so proud of you! You are very special to Jesus and me. My friend said the most incredible thing happened. Smelina just sat there and cried. She did not open the gift or lift her head. What happened next was life changing. Slowly, the bustle of people and workers in the room stopped. All eyes turned to this young girl crying holding the gift. The interpreter went over and put his hand on Smelina. He asked, "Smelina why are you crying?" Smelina simply answered, "Because I know God loves me." They were tears of joy.

Smelina got a gift that day. It was not anything material. She received much more. Knowing God loved her was the greatest gift. She looked up and smiled into the camera showing her hands proudly on top of the gift. It was as if to say, "I know God loves me just the way He made me and has great plans for my life because I am His."

This is why I love children so much. They teach us what is most important.

However I consider my life worth nothing to me; my only aim is to finish the race and complete the task the Lord Jesus has given me- the task of testifying to the good news of God's grace.

Acts 20:24

About the Author

Julia Taves has taught for over 26 years and worked as an International School Principal in the countries of Uganda and the Dominican Republic. Julia has seen God work through her own children, her students and kids across the world. Realizing these kids could be an encouragement to others, she collected writings by children with a variety of experiences, voices, and perspectives who know God's truth and want to share with other kids the things that really matter.

www.ingramcontent.com/pod-product-compliance
Lightning Source LLC
Chambersburg PA
CBHW020441130626
46549CB00001B/242